New Frontiers in Criminology

Also from Westphalia Press
westphaliapress.org

The Idea of the Digital University

France and New England Volumes 1, 2, & 3

Treasures of London

The History of Photography

L'Enfant and the Freemasons

Baronial Bedrooms

Making Trouble for Muslims

Material History and Ritual Objects

Paddle Your Own Canoe

Opportunity and Horatio Alger

Careers in the Face of Challenge

Bookplates of the Kings

Collecting American Presidential Autographs

Freemasonry in Old Buffalo

Young Freemasons?

Social Satire and the Modern Novel

The Essence of Harvard

Ivanhoe Masonic Quartettes

A Definitive Commentary on Bookplates

James Martineau and Rebuilding Theology

No Bird Lacks Feathers

Gilded Play

Earthworms, Horses, and Living Things

The Man Who Killed President Garfield

Anti-Masonry and the Murder of Morgan

Understanding Art

Homeopathy

Fishing the Florida Keys

Collecting Old Books

Masonic Secret Signs and Passwords

The Thomas Starr King Dispute

Earl Warren's Masonic Lodge

Lariats and Lassos

Mr. Garfield of Ohio

The Wisdom of Thomas Starr King

The French Foreign Legion

War in Syria

Naturism Comes to the United States

New Sources on Women and Freemasonry

Designing, Adapting, Strategizing in Online Education

Gunboat and Gun-runner

Meeting Minutes of Naval Lodge No. 4 F.A.A.M

New Frontiers in Criminology

Vol. 2, No. 1 of International Journal on Criminology

Edited by Alain Bauer

WESTPHALIA PRESS
An imprint of Policy Studies Organization

New Frontiers in Criminology: Vol. 2, No. 1 of International Journal on Criminology
All Rights Reserved © 2014 by Policy Studies Organization

Westphalia Press
An imprint of Policy Studies Organization
1527 New Hampshire Ave., NW
Washington, D.C. 20036
dgutierrezs@ipsonet.org

ISBN-13: 978-1941472903
ISBN-10: 1941472907

Updated material and comments on this edition
can be found at the Westphalia Press website:
www.westphaliapress.org

International Journal on Criminology
Volume 2 Issue 1 Spring 2014

Table of Contents

The Global Criminality Age 1
Alain Bauer

The Long Arm of Crime and Financial Crisis 5
~~Robert Cario~~

The Behavioral Intelligence Paradigm Shift in Fighting Cyber-Crime: Counter-Measures, Innovation, and Regulation Issues 11
Phillipe Baumard

Criminal State and Illicit Economy: a Game Changer for the Twenty-First Century: Crime, Illicit Trades, Economy, and State 22
Mickaël Roudaut

The Impact of Victimological Theories on the Rights of Crime Victims in France 45
Robert Cario

States of Change: Power and Counterpower Expressions in Latin America's Criminal Insurgencies 63
John P. Sullivan

The "Criminal Gang," a French Ectoplasm? 72
François Haut

Crime and Business 78
Eric Delbecque

The Global Criminality Age
Alain Bauer

To conceptualize twenty-first century crime, we need to start by setting it in a wider framework, a longer time perspective. Crime has considerable historic depth. The phenomenon is anything but new and not just a matter for large cities or national governments. Identity theft, illegal immigration, drug trafficking, terrorist attacks, human trafficking, and financial crime are developing between continents and hemispheres. Yet, there is too often a tendency to overestimate just how new these world problems are. Without a historic perspective, it is difficult to judge how the problems are changing.

The generation living just before World War I was the first to have to tackle crime on an international scale. Toward the end of the nineteenth century, governments, commentators, and opinion-makers had begun to ponder over the shrinking world ushered in by technologies and their cultural, social, and economic impact on criminal behavior. They noticed that alarming changes in ordinary criminal behavior were occurring, alongside the emergence of new forms of crime, such as anarchism, white slavery, and imported criminality. A new breed of experts that went by the name criminologists used the language of science in attempt to obtain a planetary vision of the phenomenon.

Initial Globalization of Crime

In a remarkable, little book that passed largely unnoticed, the English Professor, Paul Knepper, describes the emergence of international crime[1] in imperial Great Britain in the years between 1881 and 1914. He explores how the international dimension is the only practical way of understanding crime in Great Britain in this period and beyond. To do so, we need to look back over the progress made in transport, communication, and trade relations, resulting in an interconnected world. This is the era in which policemen, journalists, novelists, and other commentators described the rise in professional criminals and international fraudsters who used the new technologies of the age against their victims.

However, this internationalization was not purely technology-based. It also had an imperial dimension. This means that the conditions in which the political authorities of the British Empire encouraged this international-scale crime decoding work needs to be kept in mind. As a result of this, the Colonial Service turned to analogies to comprehend individuals and communities that could not be understood according to conventional patterns of thought. The "colonial" investigations resulted in comparisons between domestic criminality and the sense of a "globalized criminal class".

Fear of International Conspiracy

The process should be completed by research into migrations. In response to a wave of Anti-Semitism following the assassination of Czar Alexander II in 1881, millions of Jews fled to the West. This huge migration fostered foreign criminality, persecuting the persecuted, surfing the wave, profiting from, or revealing true self through it. Anti-Semites raised the specter

---

[1] *The Invention of International Crime—A Global Issue in the Making* (1881–1914), Palgrave

of this type of criminal behavior and stirred up fear of a population imported from within the protective borders of the Russian Empire. This led to the passing of the Aliens Act, the first legal attempt to control immigration in Great Britain and the first step toward an international policy seeking to establish identities by making passports and identity papers obligatory. The fear of foreign crime was based not only on the poverty of these communities and where they came from but on an alleged international conspiracy.

They were suspected of controlling a large portion of the "white slavery" market and trafficking in women and girls for prostitution. In fact, Jewish philanthropists invested a great deal of money in the fight against this scourge. One measure was the creation of a Jewish Association for the Protection of Women and Girls. This problem quickly attracted international attention and prompted a coordinated international response. The National Vigilance Association, founded in 1885, organized the first international conference to discuss the problem which resulted in the signature of the first international treaty on the subject in 1904. Supporters of this legal framework saw immigration, accelerated by steam ship travel, as the principle source of this scourge, coupled with the market in "artists" and the new acceptance of women moving around alone in the modern world.

A First "Londonistan"?

The assassination of the Czar in 1881 also marked the beginning of a new type of criminal behavior: the anarchist attack. In the early 1880s, anarchists or those who claimed to follow this political movement began to launch bomb attack campaigns in Europe and North America, murdering half a dozen heads of State, including US President William McKinley in 1901. London became an anarchist refuge and the era was marked by the tension produced by their presence. We could call it the first "Londonistan"… A first foiled attack was recorded in 1894 when a French anarchist was killed as he tried to destroy the Greenwich Observatory. The "International Anti-Anarchy Defense Conference" held in Rome in 1898 to respond to these threats ended without a final agreement being reached.

For the Record: Chicago and Marseille, Textbook Cases

At the end of the nineteenth century, in a developing trade in white women and other forms of international trafficking, Marseille, located at the heart of trade routes between Africa, Europe, America, and Asia, was ideally situated as a center for criminal forms of trade. The authorities became concerned about hired thugs with their tightening grip on the city. The sharp rise in drug trafficking tipped the balance: in the 1920s, this highly structured underworld, headed by gang bosses, their enforcers and henchmen, and governed by its traditions (the law of silence) prospered with the help of rampant police force corruption, close ties between criminals and local politicians and, above all, a boom in alcohol and drug trafficking. Marseille became the nerve center of the trade between North America (an important growth area for consumption) and Asia (for production). Although for a long time, the leading Western countries and Japan took on a role of "lawful dealers", waging an opium war to reestablish the drug trade in China despite it having recently been outlawed there (between 1839 and 1842, then 1856 and 1860), changing attitudes were fuelling a trend toward prohibition almost everywhere and led to the signature, in January 1912, of the first international drug control treaty, the Hague International Opium Convention.

In 1925, the "Marseille Godfathers", Paul Carbone and François Spirito (one Italian, the other Corsican) held a meeting in Egypt. They formed a prostitution, trafficking, racketeering, and extortion partnership and invented the first case of criminal activity "industrialization" in the West. The first factories producing heroine from opium imported raw from Indochina, and later Turkey (processed in France and distributed in the United States) were established in Marseille in 1937. In Chicago, Alfonse Capone took full advantage of the perverse effects of Prohibition, investing in the bootlegging of black market alcohol and industrial-scale money laundering. Following the purest rules of an advanced free-market economy, they set up business on the shores of the Mediterranean and on the other side of the Atlantic, practiced vertical and horizontal integration, invested in research and development, developed staff incentives, extended their trade areas, and engaged in tax planning. Their treatment of their competitors seems to be the only facet of their business that was a great deal more "final" than in honest sectors of the economy.

At the time of the French Liberation, their successors, the Guérini brothers, who were more successful in their choice of political allies during the Occupation, made new alliances, extending their empire and diversifying their businesses, investing in cigarette smuggling to supplement their international narcotics trade, swelled by their close relationship with the New York Godfather, Lucky Luciano. The French Connection was born. The first international trading agreement for the distribution of industrially-produced heroine was made in the 1960s.

In Marseille, it took the Liberation to end the Carbone and Spirito Empire. It was taken over by the Guérini Brothers whose political alliances had been more astute. In Chicago, Elliott Ness, a Prohibition Bureau agent, put an end to Capone's career with charges of tax evasion. Franck Nitti, then Tony Accardo, took over operations without great difficulty, but with less provocation and lower visibility.

The Guérini Brothers lost their stranglehold over Marseille at the beginning of the 1960s, after their attempt, with others, to extend their hold over Parisian gaming circles. The result was the "gambling war" of the mid-1960s, resulting in Antoine's murder and Barthélémy's imprisonment. A new figure, Gaëtan Zampa, then came onto the scene. Marseille became the setting for a bloody gang war. In 1972–1973, Zampa's ambitions clashed with the aspirations of Francis Vanverberghe, or "Francis Le Belge", who was deeply involved in narcotics trafficking. The conflict resulted in bloody street battles resulting in many deaths but creating the heyday of the "scandal papers" until Zampa's arrest and imprisonment in November 1983.

The first decade of this century was particularly dark for the Marseille underworld. On September 27, 2000, Francis Le Belge, who had taken the Marseille Mafia in hand despite living in Paris, was murdered. Two years after his death, the Marseille criminal scene burst into violence in a merciless war between gypsy criminals, for a time led by Farid Berrahma, the "Rôtisseur", Corsicans from Bastia and homegrown criminals from Marseille. The increasing competition between rival gangs led to revenge murders and reckonings but they were also fuelled by the ever-younger protagonists involved in these rousts, who lacked the professionalism, cool composure, and code of conducts of the old Mafia Godfathers.

Since then, the blows inflicted by the police to a number of gangs (arrest of the Campanella Brothers and Bernard Barresi in 2010 and imprisonment of Jacques Cassandri in January 2011) have helped to open the way to other groups from the housing projects. They are waging outright war to safeguard their territory and protect their business interests.

A war of succession and a war of secession are being waged simultaneously, which, with the accidental death of Jean Gé Colonna, the last gangland peace mediator, has resulted in the fragmentation of the local criminal territory.

There have been similar developments in the United States with the arrival of powerful criminal gangs from Latin America, including Mexico and Guatemala. As is often the case, there is evidence of a "postcolonial" effect on changes to the criminal environment.

Therefore, without us realizing it, globalization and crime have progressed together, at first in parallel and later through direct cross-connections, with each fuelling the other. The era of international criminal behavior is now in full flow.

Unfortunately, in criminal matters, like terrorism, which is just another facet of crime, the new is too often just the forgotten.

Yet, it is still possible to be surprised. Controlling territories, conquering other spaces, attracting attention through bullying and bragging, provoking governments like Capone or Escobar, creating strategies of fear through the murders of General Della Chiesa, or judges Borsellino and Falcone, before adopting a lower profile, criminal organizations, especially in the financial sector, have learned how to be forgotten.

However, more recently, some have taken another path of "freeing up" entire regions to create "Narco-States". On an entirely different scale to petty score-settling, there is a higher level of conflict mobilizing veritable armies: criminal warfare.

The Long Arm of Crime and Financial Crisis
Alain Bauer

Starting with the "Yakuza recession" of the 1980s, then the U.S. Savings and Loans Crisis of the same era, followed by Mexico, Russia, and Thailand, a series of financial crises with a more or less marked criminal dimension has rocked the world's leading countries over the last 30 years. Central regulators paid no attention to this phenomenon despite International Monetary Fund (IMF) estimates of a quantity of dirty cash of between 1% and 5% of world gross domestic product (GDP). The world of crime has become a financier of primary importance.

The Savings and Loans Hold Up

The Savings and Loans Crisis devastated U.S. savings associations in the 1980s. Almost two thirds of these institutions went out of business through bankruptcies that were clearly fraudulent. The crisis is estimated to have cost around US$160 billion, US$124.6 billion of which was doled out by the U.S. Treasury, a cost equivalent to World War II.[1]

Jean-François Gayraud reminds us that, according to the U.S. General Accounting Office (the federal accounts auditing body) and to the numerous judicial, university, and journalistic investigations conducted since, these bankruptcies resulted from massive and systematic misappropriations carried out from inside the savings associations themselves by senior executives (white collar crime), sometimes in association with members of traditional gangland groups.

Effective governance of these "thrift" associations had become lax. The Garn-St Germain Depository Institutions Act 1982 had deregulated the sector regardless of its particular sensitivity to criminal ambitions. Local Mafias leapt into the breach. Based on falsified documents, an increasing number of loans at very low interest rates were granted to "friends" on very "flexible" terms and conditions. At the same time, a systematic use of "creative" accounting concealed the colossal losses. In 1987, the U.S. Attorney General acknowledged massive frauds.

The vast majority of the ill-gotten gains raked in by the fraudsters were secreted away into tax havens. It also led to the collapse of the U.S. construction market, which fell from 1.8 million new homes per year to only 1 million between 1986 and 1991.

"Yakuza Recession"[2]

The Japanese "Yakusa" are some of the most powerful organized crime organizations. In 2008, there were nearly 90,000 members amalgamated into

---

[1] On this crisis see (in French) Jean-François Gayraud, "*Crises Financières: la Dimension Criminelle*" (Financial Crises, the Criminal Dimension), *Défense Nationale et Sécurité Collective*, December 2008; Jean-François Gayraud, "*La Dimension Criminelle de la Crise des Subprimes*" (The Criminal Dimension in the Subprime Crisis), *Diplomatie*, Special Edition No. 8, April–May 2009 and (in English) Kitty Calavita, Henry N. Pontell, and Robert H. Tillman, "*Big Money Crime, Fraud and Politics in the Savings and Loan Crisis*", University of California Press, 1997.

[2] On this crisis see Jean-François Gayraud, "*Le Monde des Mafias, Géopolitique du Crime Organisé*" (The Mafia World, Geopolitics of Organized Crime) (Odile Jacob, 2005 and 2008); Jean-François Gayraud, Crises Financières: *la Dimension Criminelle* (Financial Crises, the Criminal Dimension), *Défense Nationale et Sécurité Collective*, December 2008.

three leading criminal federations (Inagawa kai, Yamaguchi Gumi, and Sumiyoshi Rengo). These organizations are involved in the usual array of crimes: racketeering and protection, arms trafficking, prostitution, pornography, illegal gaming (Pachinko), and merchandise smuggling.

During the 1980s, the "Jusen" (real estate lending cooperatives) were frequent victims of falsified loans, many of which were applied for by companies "reeking" of Yakuza involvement. According to the Japanese government, in 1999 alone, more than 40% of loans to finance construction found themselves in the hands of organized crime syndicates. In 2002, it was estimated that there were still "bad loans" (Mafia loans, for the most part) valued at between US$800 and US$1600 billion. According to Japan's national police force, around half of these "bad loans" were non-recoverable as they were held by organized crime. Goldman Sachs confirmed the estimate in relation to business loans. According to the TV channel, NHK, two in five Japanese companies had Yakuza links. After inflating the market, the Yakuza bought up real estate assets at slashed prices and forcibly blocked settlement of the liabilities of some companies. The rare bankers who dared to intervene were threatened and, in some cases, murdered.

The extraordinary duration of the Japanese financial crisis, despite the many and far-reaching recovery measures, can only be understood if the criminal dimension is included in the equation. The Yakuza caused companies to absorb losses from the unpaid loans and then privatized Mafia profits.

The country has still not recovered.

"The Collape of the Russia House"[3]

The transition to a market economy in the Russian Federation began at the end of 1991. In 1992, Russia launched a massive privatization program. "Shock therapy" began in 1994 with 50% of the public sector organizations (i.e., more than 100,000 State enterprises) being privatized. This fast-paced deregulation of the economy was conducted in highly questionable circumstances.

The privatizations and control over raw materials for the most part benefitted businessmen with close connections to the Leadership. The country witnessed a grabbing of public assets, monopolized by a group of cronies. These new "robber barons" acquired notoriety and became known as the "oligarchs". These profiteers, sometimes backed by a criminal underworld in full revival, realized that their situation was precarious and invested their ill-gotten gains abroad in tax and banking havens.

Through these "hasty" privatizations, the transition initially caused the GDP to halve. Unemployment, at a rate of less than 0.1% of the working population at the start of the 1990s, rose to 7.5% in 1994. At the same time, according to the Lancet (2009), the mortality rate increased four times faster in Russia than in other benchmark countries.

The economic depression culminated in the financial crisis of 1998, marked by sharp devaluation in the rouble and a sovereign debt default. The flight of capital via criminal activity during this period is estimated at US$100 billion.

A large portion of the funds injected into the country's economy by international institutions such as the IMF and the

---

[3] On this transition see Joseph Stiglitz, "*Quand le Capitalisme Perd la Tête*" (When Capitalism Loses its Head) (Fayard 2003); Joseph Stiglitz, *La Grande Désillusion* (Globalization and its Discontents) (Fayard 2002).

World Bank to save it from the damaging effects of the "shock therapy" was diverted and placed outside Russia.

"The Tequila Crisis" 1994

The 1994–1995 Mexican financial crisis, known as the "Tequila Effect" was, more than anything, a "cocaine effect". Mexican traffickers acquired a very large share in the revenues from Colombian drugs exported to the United States at the beginning of the 1990s, earning themselves more than US$10 billion per year. The business privatizations under the Salinas presidency (1988–1994) provided an opportunity for "recycling" the profits from narcotics through a banking sector that had itself been privatized. Following the 1994–1995 crisis, the banks owed more than US$180 billion for which the State Treasury was forced to assume liability.

Combined with an influx of international capital, this money laundering contributed to a massive injection of enormous sums of cash into the economy and the creation of a double real estate and stock market "bubble". Although they represented only 1% to 3% of Mexican GDP in the beginning, both in trade and in banking, the narcotics dollars distorted markets in favor of Mafia networks. The "money laundering premium" earned by the drugs barons made them more competitive and able to "absorb" their competitors and yet still focus on short-term speculative investments. Access to credit enabled them to recycle dirty capital and to increase the power of its impact. The injection of narcotics dollars weakened trade and precipitated payment defaults, causing the Peso to be devalued and bringing on the financial crisis. It cost the Mexican Treasury more than US$100 billion and increased unemployment threefold.

"The Thai Bubble"

The 1997 Asian Crisis started in Thailand, where the scenario was a similar one. The equivalent of 10% of Thai GDP was controlled by organized crime networks which earned their income for the most part from illegal gaming, prostitution, and trafficking in drugs exported from Burma. As in Mexico, the influx of short-term foreign capital accelerated a speculative trend. The deterioration in external accounts made worse by the increase in the value of the US dollar and shrinkage of expert opportunities precipitated the devaluation of the Baht.

However, the local political and financial system also played a role by massively encouraging the laundering of illegal and Mafia earnings. At the end of 1999, despite a 10% fall in Thai GDP in 1998 and real estate overcapacity in Bangkok estimated at more than three hundred thousand units, sales prices held their ground. The reason for this stability, impossible to comprehend in market terms, becomes clear if we consider the money laundering circuit impact.

---

[4] On this crisis see a number of articles by Jean-François Gayraud: "*La Dimension Criminelle de la Crise des Subprimes* (The Criminal Dimension of the Subprime Crisis), *Diplomatie*, Special Edition No. 8, April–May 2009; "*Crises Financières: la Dimension Criminelle Un An Après*" (Financial Crises, the Criminal Dimension One year On), *Défense Nationale et Sécurité Collective,* December 2009; "*Capitalisme Criminel: Subprimes ou Subcrimes?*" (Criminal Capitalism: Subprime or Subcrime?), Cité, No. 41, PUF, March 2010.

[5] See Noël Pons, "*La Crise des Subprimes: une Aubaine pour les Criminalités?*" (Subprime Crisis: A Bonanza for Criminals), Cahiers de la Sécurité, No. 7, January–March 2009.

"The Subprime Tsunami"[4]

As highlighted by the expert, Noël Pons[5], the mechanics of the crisis that broke out in 2009 were almost identical to that of the 1980s. Only the parties involved were different. In this new format, the banks were fed with applications for loans by mortgage brokers who made lavish promises. A number of applications were discreetly categorized as "non-documented". They were in fact faked, involving acts of fraud, scamming, abuse of trust, and forgery. Operating with the backing of mortgage lenders, the brokers dispensed questionable loans, using predatory lending techniques, consisting of lending to people from vulnerable demographic groups (poor people, ethnic minorities, etc.). Credit frequently exceeded 125% of the value of the home purchased with the loan. Home values were also significantly inflated. Loans were frequently made to borrowers unable to meet capital repayments on an interest only basis, a system thriving only in conditions of speculation. The illusion persists as long as the market is still rising. The entire economy, steeped in debt, became a "pyramid economy", a gigantic Ponzi scheme.

In an attempt to conceal what was really happening, the banks tried amalgamating loans into common pools by "securitizing" them and then, in the second stage, mixing the "junk" securities with others in global structures, themselves overvalued, to produce a cocktail of fund derivatives based on nothing, but still highly speculative. Naturally, accounts were also falsified or externalized. In the third stage, the "globalized" structures were insured and then reinsured and finally sold to "investors", many of whom were domiciled in tax havens. These on-sold "receivables" were then used as leverage to raise loans from the major commercial banks that placed these "virtual securities" with other, notably foreign, banks, local authorities, associations, etc. From the bottom of the ladder upwards, these dealings may not always have been blatantly fraudulent but were at least often very shady.

A few months before the outbreak of the subprime crisis, although nothing could be done to prevent it, Michael Mukasey, Attorney General in the George W. Bush administration, curiously denounced the criminalization of the economic and financial markets on April 23, 2008, at a conference on organized crime at the Center for Strategic and International Studies (CSIS).

More recently in Europe, there was the case of *the carbon VAT scam which involved buying rights to pollute, exclusive of VAT, in one European country through a dummy or shell company, with almost immediate resale on the French, English, or Italian markets, inclusive of VAT. The fraudsters pocket the VAT rate differential and disperse it between offshore accounts.*

These transactions involve the fraudsters themselves, their protectors, and financiers, especially the "launderers" of the monies earned from trafficking, including in narcotics. A judge was reported in the newspaper "Le Parisian" as saying that *"there is a veritable Mafia behind the carbon emissions tax and a Mafia does not hesitate to kill."*

In January 2009, Serge Lepage, son of a well-known underground figure, was shot down in front of his home. It was suspected that he had been called upon as a provider of funding for carbon emission tax fraudsters.

Amar Azzoug was executed on April 30, 2010, in a brasserie in Saint-Mandé. A known former bank robber, this 35-year-old man had been implicated in carbon tax fraud and its embezzled millions. He had known that he was a marked man and had alerted the police, incriminating Samy Souied as the probable person behind the threats.

Five months later, Samy Souied himself was shot down by two men in front of the Palais des Congrès at Porte Maillot in Paris. He had just landed from Tel Aviv and was due to leave again that same evening. He was carrying €300,000 in cash. The last man who had spoken to him was the former son-in-law of Claude Dray, a hugely-wealthy businessman and art collector, murdered at his mansion house in Neuilly-sur-Seine on the night of October 24/25, 2011.

There was nothing that seemingly connected this murder with the previous ones. However, his assassination does raise questions: his safe was full of jewels and other valuables but nothing was stolen.

The real gangland bosses are concealed behind these "white collar" swindlers and fraudsters. These men do not forgive errors or oversights. Similarly, the "loveable rogues" of old were not inclined to forgive, and the amounts of money at stake explain this epidemic of old-fashioned 7.65 mm weapon murders.

At the beginning of February 2012, the French Court of Auditors covered this affair in its annual report. It stated "*the carbon emission quota VAT fraud is the largest tax fraud ever recorded in France in so short a time. It demonstrates failings in regulating a market in which naivety about how resourceful fraudsters can be combines with risk perception errors on the part of market administrators and government. It also highlights the inadequacy in forward planning to provide effective regulation tools for markets in which, given their characteristics, the fraud potential has been overlooked.*"

The Court of Auditors assessed the tax loss to the French autumn 2008 to June 2009 budget at €1.6 billion. Europol estimated the total loss within the European Union at €5 billion. Twenty or so prosecutions have now been brought involving more than a hundred individuals.

"*Neither the European Commission nor Member States have shown any concern for safeguarding the conditions in which the VAT is collected*", stated the Court, which underscored "*the original flaws and loopholes in the system: almost unrestricted access by any natural person or corporate entity to national quota registers and the lack of external regulation.*" It also criticized the "*inadequate vigilance on the part of the market administrator, too superficial an applicant identity checking process, unconvincing application of duties of vigilance, market operators perceived the systemic magnitude of the fraud too late, errors and mismanagement on the part of finance ministries.*" On the subject of TRACFIN, the French financial intelligence unit, the Court of Auditors noted "*data processing delays incompatible with swift action to stop fraud*". It also criticized the General Directorate for Public Finance for failing to "*anticipate*" the magnitude of the fraud, stressing that "*its standard procedures were not fit for purpose*" and "*there was inadequate coordination between its different services.*"

Despite acknowledging the May 2009 decision by the Finance Ministry to alter the VAT collection method on CO_2 quota transactions to stem Treasury losses, the Court of Auditors reiterated the point that there were still "*persistent problems, especially of poor*" or inadequate control of access to registers.

In short, as usual, the commission of enquiry only exposed what had been known for a long time (the first frauds of this type date back to the 1970s): slow-moving and cumbersome regulatory authority action; existing systems incapable of taking the criminal dimension into account.

Criminal organizations started on a small-scale to test the market, just a few hundred thousand francs to begin with. Yet, they have managed to steal several billion euros with 40 years of practical experience, like the Ponzi schemes that will soon celebrate a century of existence, and which still seem as effective as ever. What will the next stage be?

The Behavioral Intelligence Paradigm Shift in Fighting Cyber-Crime: Counter-Measures, Innovation, and Regulation Issues

Phillipe Baumard

This paper investigates the technological evolution of cyber-crimes from its emergence in the early 1980s to its latest developments in 2013. From this evolution, we draw implications for doctrines, policy, innovation, incentives, and roadmaps as we propose the emergence of a new "behavioral intelligence" paradigm, both in the attack and defense arenas.

Cyber-crime refers to the unlawful use of numeric, electronic, and software capabilities to misuse, temper, devoid, destruct, or influence public or private information systems. Cybernetic and informational components may not be the primary target or final outcomes of cyber-crime campaigns.

The origins of cyber-crime are concomitant with the pioneering efforts of technology enthusiasts in exploring the possibilities offered by technological innovation. Exploration and autonomous appropriation are still, to date, a core motivation in the creation of "hacks". John Draper was one of these computer enthusiasts who helped popularize the first "phreaking" hack, consisting of a multi-frequency tone generator, later known as the Blue Box to pitch the exact 2600 Hz frequency to hack into the long distance phone system of AT&T in the early 1970s.

Most of the early attacks were spontaneous, motivated by technology exploration, non-directed (without a specific target in mind), and immediate in their effects. With the rise of personal computers, these early pioneers of hacking started to group in spontaneous associations, espousing discourses of the times on individual freedom, resistance to authority, and amusement with detours of emerging technologies. Phreaking and hacking became both shared practices that cemented long friendships between developers, industry pioneers (Wozniak, Jobs, etc.), and politically motivated technology enthusiasts. The borders between an emerging underground culture (yippies and hackers) and a criminal sub-culture were blurry and unstable, with very little self-regulation, and comprising teenagers, advanced computer developers, and self-taught technology explorers. We call this era the "code breaking years", where talented individuals are mostly motivated by symbolic and small gains, a feeling of belonging to a new community and self-identity.

However, in the mid-1980s, technical bulletin boards from hackers' groups started to disclose attack guidelines for intrusions, sometimes both physical and code-based (such as the first issue of the Legion of Doom LOD/H Technical Journal, on Jan. 1, 1987). LOD and MOD (Masters of Deception) hence became influential in transforming these early movements into more organized "cracking" communities, moving a step away from the original hacking culture (see Figure 1).

[A] Professor, *Ecole Polytechnique*, Chair Innovation and Regulation of Numerical Services

[1] http://www.textfiles.com/magazines/LOD/lod-1

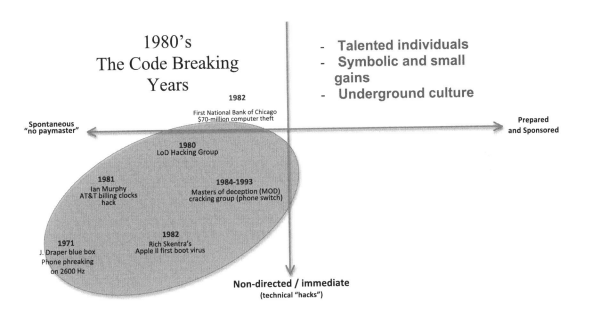

Figure 1. The early years: the code-breaking paradigm

The Cold War and the underground battle for a free Berlin played a determinant role in the evolution of the hacking culture of the late 1980s. The Clifford Stoll episode (an LBL astronomer who accidentally discovered a computer intrusion from West Germany in his laboratory) was the first case to raise the importance of agency coordination and the difficulties of attribution in international computer attacks (Stoll 1989). This case is also one of the early symptoms (1986) of yet to come advanced persistent threats, highlighting the complexity and sophistication of intrusion campaigns (for details see Stoll's article, 1988[2]).

The early 1990s are hence concomitant with the emergence of the criminal sub-culture of hacking. In the 1980s, cracking events that led to theft or large-scale attacks were rare. Two notable exceptions are the 1986 Pak Brain logic bomb, known as the first virus, and the 1982 First National Bank of Chicago computer theft ($70 M USD). The "Great Hacker War" (conflict between Masters of Deception and Legion of Doom, circa 1991–1992) is an example—today disputed as an exaggeration of trivial confrontations—of the interpersonal dynamics of the early 1990s. A blend of prestige seeking, bravados, and playfulness were the core incentives of these early confrontations[3]. The publication of exploits by hackers' groups triggered, however, the interest of Law enforcement. Operation Sundevil, in 1990, was hence the first large-scale cyber-enforcement operation, involving 15 U.S. cities and leading to three arrests[4]. Most cyber-crimes involved wire-tapping, calling card fraud, and credit card fraud.

The relative failure of this operation led to an increased awareness of the central role of cyber-deterrence for federal agencies (Sterling 1994).

Publications such as 2600 and the rise of the cyber-space participate in a democratization of cracking, phreaking, and hacking techniques, which render them more versatile to their use "beyond technology". Focus on distant control, resident threats (democratization of Trojans) creates both a more organized criminal sub-culture, and the birth of a societal reach for the attacks (see Figure 2).

While attack preparation is targeted to single point of aggression, the early 2000s is adopting a whole new dynamic. The rise of electronic commerce means a better monetization of cyber-crime with an expectation of large-scale profits for organized crime. The digitalization of the cultural industry (MP3s) creates an appeal for the popular growth of cracking. Profiles of hackers accordingly change in two directions: on the one hand, amateur crackers (script kiddies and mass market consumers) start to use without advanced knowledge available tools (P2P file sharing and cracking "CDs"). On the other hand, malware production becomes a profitable black market. Corruption of DNS paths, denial-of-service attacks, defacing campaigns, and corporate thefts find a rapid monetization. The years 2000–2002 are among the most active in malware generation with viruses such as ILOVEYOU, Klez.h., Code Red, etc. The group Anonymous is created in 2003 as a loosely coupled and spontaneous coordination of various interests, ranging from militant activism, cracking

---

[2] http://pdf.textfiles.com/academics/wilyhacker.pdf

[3] http://www.textfiles.com/hacking/modbook4.txt

[4] Anthony Lawrence Clapes, *Softwars: The Legal Battles for Control of the Global Software Industry*. (Westport, CT: Quorum Books, 1993).

International Journal on Criminology

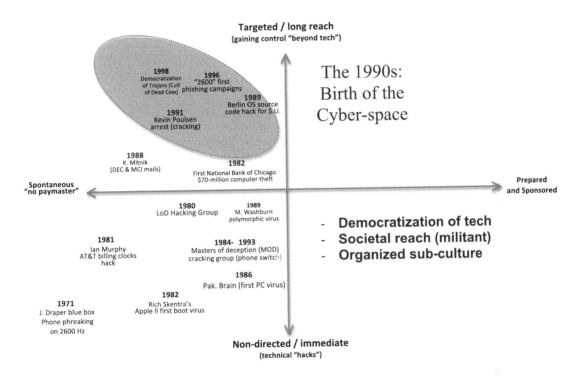

Figure 2. The 1990s: the democratization of cyber-crime

techniques sharing, and image sharing around the 4chan platform. Massive raids and pranks, known as "4chan raids", popularize a perspective of hacking as a blend of activism, bullying, and satirist information campaigns, although opting out of political campaigns in the early years (2003–2006).

Meanwhile, preparation and sponsorship of large-scale attacks also gain considerable traction as the core philosophy of hacking (based on freedom and activism values) is fading away with the diffusion of embedded cracking tools and libraries. Titan Rain (2003–2006) is an exemplar of these first explorations of cyber-warfare involving low-tech methodologies embedded into advanced campaigns (see Figure 3).

The years 2005–2013 are marked by a double shift, and to some extent a seizure, between "target and sponsored campaigns" led by States or organized crime, and more pervasive "spontaneous and long-reach campaigns" led by activist groups, hackers' collectives, and loosely coupled entities such as Anonymous and LulzSec. This period is characterized by a rapid growth of strategic and politically motivated attacks (Kerem125 against the United Nations, Chinese APT1 global campaign, Estonia DoS attacks, Stuxnet, and Operation Aurora) (Figure 4).

The technology used in these large-scale campaigns does not dramatically differ from the early days of hacking. One hundred and twenty-five lines of codes are still very efficient in 2013 to conduct the exploitation of vulnerabilities, even when the lines of defense have exponentially grown in the past 25 years. As most innovation disruptions in the early twenty-first century, the performance of these campaigns is rooted in the accessibility and diffusion of combinatory learning, i.e., the capacity of outpacing the defensive learning of targets by a better and faster behavioral intelligence.

The formation of two distinctive groups (large-scale spontaneous groups versus sponsored targeted large-scale campaigns) is typical of the two paths that can be used to attain a superior collective behavioral learning advantage. Large spontaneous groups benefit from distributed astute learning, i.e., the learning conducted by individual hackers who can coordinate on a very large scale, making their collective learning ubiquitous and efficient. Targeted sponsored campaigns (such as APTs) benefit from the advance of automated artificial intelligence embedded into technology (e.g., Stuxnet and FLAME).

Most defensive systems are based on the recognition of signatures ("embedded malicious codes") of malwares, or on the normative analysis of behaviors compared to "healthy behaviors" (knowledge-based detection systems). Both the collective learning of spontaneous groups and advanced machine learning currently outpace signature-based detection systems. The nature of the current paradigm shift is, in this sense, very similar to the evolution of information warfare in the early 1990s. We are witnessing a strategic disruption where defenders are consolidating their information infrastructures, while attackers are engaging in knowledge-warfare (Baumard 1994). Superior knowledge, through astute combination, can be gained from truncated and partial information. Superior information rarely defeats even poorly articulated knowledge.

A *behavioral intelligence paradigm* is synonymous with an inescapable rise of "zero days" threats. Pervasive and highly available combinatory learning allows the creation of many variants of an exploit (exploitation of a vulnerability) within 24 hours of its discovery. Re-encapsulating and re-combining the exploits of undiscovered flaws ("zero days") is made possible

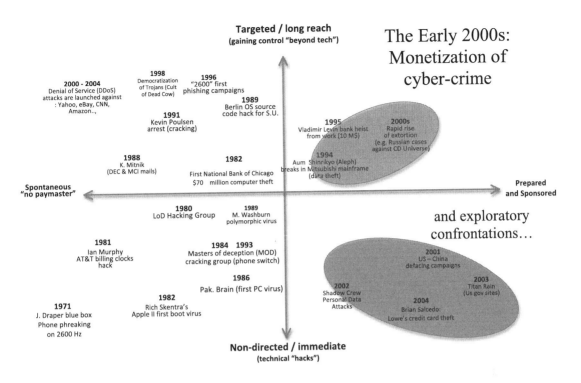

Figure 3. The monetization of cyber-crime and first State confrontations

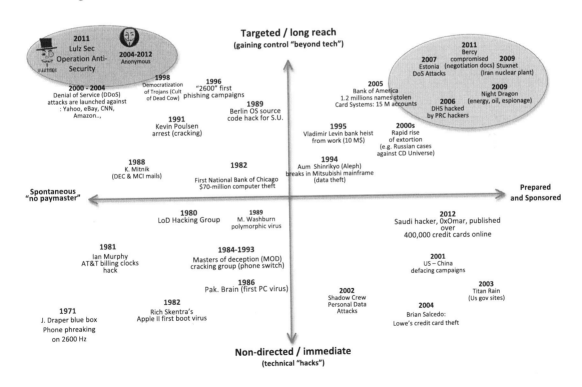

Figure 4. Beyond technology: the rise of large-scale targeted campaigns (2005–2013)

by the advancement of causative learning techniques, or when inaccessible, by the very large number of spontaneous hacking groups sharing their recombination experiments. In such a paradigm, focusing on ex-post defense strategy based on known and identified vulnerabilities is likely to fail.

Putting contemporary doctrines to the test of technological shifts

By gathering data from public sources on published Cyber-Defense doctrines, we try in the second part of this analysis to assess the soundness of Cyber-Doctrines for the deterrence of behavioral intelligence-driven threats. We analyzed 38 national strategies to fight cyber-crime, implement cyber-defense, and promote resilient information infrastructures and cyber-security.

We used the framework developed earlier on the history of cyber-criminality to categorize four categories of cyber-crimes, based on their destination ("targeted and long-reach" versus "immediate or non-directed") and their preparation ("spontaneous" versus "prepared and sponsored"). Hence, we identify four classes of cyber-crime: "code warriors" (I), "cyber free riders" (II), "autonomous collectives" (III), and "sponsored attackers" (IV).

Different classes of attacks require different responses. Immediate and spontaneous attacks (Class I) can be handled with robust information security, including causative learning that can deter sophisticated AI attacks. Most national doctrines have a sound understanding and appropriate range of responses for such attacks. Prepared and sponsored immediate attacks (computer theft by organized crime, free-riding, phishing, and cracking—Class II) require a coordinated range of technical and jurisdictional responses. Signature-based detection systems and knowledge-based defenses are usually sufficient to deter most threats, as far as regulation is judicially enforced. Socially and society-rooted attacks (hactivist groups, temporary or goal-driven groups with political, societal, or economic motives—Class III) involve perception warfare, information warfare, and sense-making capabilities so as to respond to rapid and emergent distributed deployment. Finally, offensive campaigns with embedded behavioral intelligence (Class IV) require transversal responses that encompass proactive deterrence "beyond tech" and "beyond claim". Class III and Class IV threats call for real-time sense-making on unprecedented scales, involving large-scale human cognitive learning on one side (III) and large-scale behavioral learning on the other side (IV).

Our analysis of the evolution of national cyber-crime doctrines over the period 1994–2013 brings mixed findings. *"Power-sovereign" doctrines* (P-S, Class IV) emphasize the development of large specialized units, are often obsessed with critical infrastructures protection, and develop more or less publicly, offensive capabilities. While they deliver sustainable deterrence policies on State-sponsored cyber attacks, they usually develop a threat-rigidity dominant logic, which impedes their involvement in emergent societal change. The risk for P-S doctrines is therefore disconnecting with emergent hacking movements, and a lack of reactivity to distributed cognitive warfare. *"Societal Resilience" doctrines* (Class III), on the other hand, are more sensitive to opinion movements, try to leverage the public space, and focus their offensive capabilities on information warfare. Motivation for such doctrines is not always rooted in a democratic and progressive view of the Internet. Yet, the digitalization of society is clearly identified as both the core threat and core opportunity for cyber-defense and cyber-development.

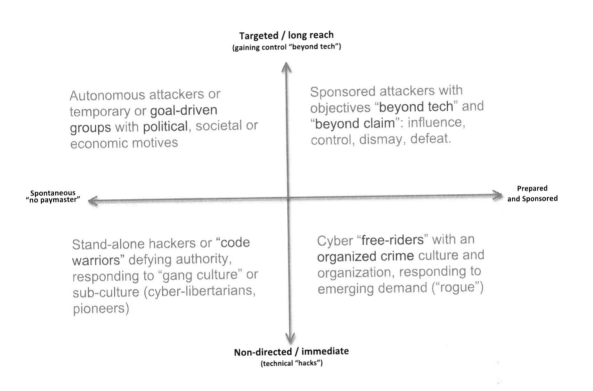

Figure 5

Finally, "Social order" doctrines (Class I) and "Technocratic" doctrines (Class II) only differ in their perception of control. The main difference lies in a control at the source (I) versus a control by a normalization of the outputs (II). Technocratic perspectives often suffer from a delayed perception of technological change, mainly inspired by an incident-response philosophy or a late entry to the field. Doctrines that favor social order generally suffer from a lack of national vision or national strategy, or have built their policies by borrowing (or aligning to) external national visions.

The following graph presents the positioning of different national cyber-crime deterrence and cyber-defense strategies (year indicates date of first document analyzed). The findings illustrate the trade-off between national policies that focused on organized cyber-crime and policies driven by the surveillance (or the support) of the societal rooting of cyber-developments. Interestingly, the Russian cyber-doctrine is closer to emergent societal developments than its Chinese or U.S. counterparts.

Measuring the robustness of national strategies: what to expect?

Most of the studied national strategies derive their national cyber criminality deterrence with an average delay of 10–15 years with the advancement of technology. Accordingly, society-wide disruptions have been systematically overlooked. Typically, cyber-policies grow in the fxourth class, while the most disruptive change is taking place in the third.

Core hacking technologies have been steadily stable in the 1990–2012 period. Advanced Persistent Threats (APTs) are not *per se* the result of a disruption in core exploits, but rather a paradigmatic change coming from peripheral technologies (mainly machine learning, automation, and combinatory reconfiguration). Such a paradigmatic change thrives on the obsolescence of an aging infrastructure. Combinations are made possible when flaws can be exploited cross-systems. The growing interoperability of vulnerable systems increases the probability of the on-the-fly exploitation of cross-vulnerabilities. In such a context, vendors, by pushing cyber-criminality deterrence to focus on "points of access" vulnerability assessment impede investment in behavioral learning technologies (by maintaining a poorly performing, but highly profitable, signature-based defense paradigm).

The only way to counteract and deter intelligent behaviors is by outpacing and outsmarting its behavioral intelligence. Very few studied doctrines have acknowledged this core systemic vulnerability. Confidence building and security measures (CBSMs) are hence rooted in a technological and societal understanding that may foster vulnerabilities, and suffer from a critical blind spot on the nature of future technological threats.

Technocratic (Class II) and social order (Class I) national doctrines are dependent on vertical and jurisdictional knowledge, while the evolution of threats is horizontal and a-jurisdictional. Most recent large-scale campaigns (APT1, Blaster-worm, etc.) have shown the limits of inter-jurisdictional coordination in responding to attacks with unpredictable attribution, unknown or undiscovered signatures, and using causative learning to adapt to common technical responses.

Most of the analyzed doctrines presented an outdated perception of authorship and attribution. Attribution is assimilated in most doctrines with a geographical point of emission (or several), a central intent, and a legalist perspective on tracking back attacks.

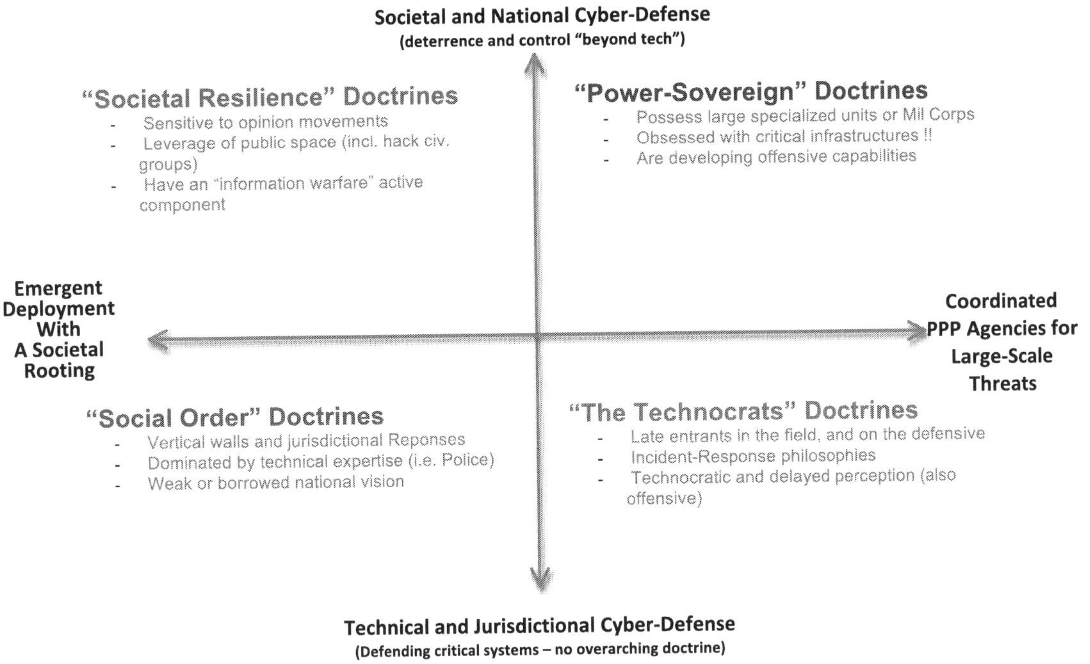

Societal and National Cyber-Defense
(deterrence and control "beyond tech")
"Societal Resilience" Doctrines
- Sensitive to opinion movements
- Leverage of public space (incl. hack civ. groups)
- Have an "information warfare" active component
"Power-Sovereign" Doctrines
- Possess large specialized units or Mil Corps
- Obsessed with critical infrastructures !!
- Are developing offensive capabilities
Emergent Deployment With A Societal Rooting
Coordinated PPP Agencies for Large-Scale Threats
"Social Order" Doctrines
- Vertical walls and jurisdictional Reponses
- Dominated by technical expertise (i.e. Police)
- Weak or borrowed national vision
"The Technocrats" Doctrines
- Late entrants in the field, and on the defensive
- Incident-Response philosophies
- Technocratic and delayed perception (also offensive)
Technical and Jurisdictional Cyber-Defense
(Defending critical systems – no overarching doctrine)

Figure 6

Societal and National Cyber-Defense
(deterrence and control "beyond tech")
2005 SINGAPORE "Infocom Security Master plan"
2005 JAPAN NISC + Self-Defense
2006 FINLAND "Strategy for Security in Society"
2007 ESTONIA Defense League and citizen involvement
1997 RUSSIA FSB + Academia
2001 ISRAEL Md + Matzov + Shin Bet National Cyber Taskforce
2004 CHINA People Liberation Army Air Force special corps
2009 GERMANY National Cyberdefense
1996 USA NCRCG + cyber command
2009 AUSTRALIA Cyber-Security Strategy (public – private)
2005 ARGENTINA Computer Science Troops (US aligned)
2010 NORWAY Education + awareness
2010 TURKEY Cyber-Command
1997 KOREA Schools + CWC
2012 Netherlands PPP + best practices
2007 PAKISTAN NRC cyber-crimes
2005 SERBIA Cyber Crime Dept
2009 UK CSOC + OCSIA
2008 AUSTRIA Electronic Defense
2005 INDIA DIWA +NTIC +DRDO
Emergent Deployment With A Societal Rooting
Coordinated PPP Agencies for Large-Scale Threats
2010 CANADA Cyber-Security Strategy (education and CIS)
2008 BRAZIL National Strategy of Defense
2008 FRANCE Livre Blanc PPP and CIS
2007 MALAYSIA "CyberSecurity Malaysia"
2011 UAE Emirates Emergency Responses
2005 COLOMBIA Interagency and CERT based
2010 BELARUS Information Confrontation Military Doctrine
2011 SWEDEN Incident Response
2010 LITHUANIA NATO-Based
2003 ITALY Cyber-crime unit (Carabinieri)
2011 POLAND NATO-based
2008 DENMARK Defense-centric
2009 IRAN Islamic R Guard cyber corps (2400)
2005 NORTH KOREA Offensive Army Units
2009 SWITZERLAND Cert-based doctrine
2010 ALBANIA IMOC
2005 GEORGIA National Security Concept
Technical and Jurisdictional Cyber-Defense
(Defending critical systems – no overarching doctrine)

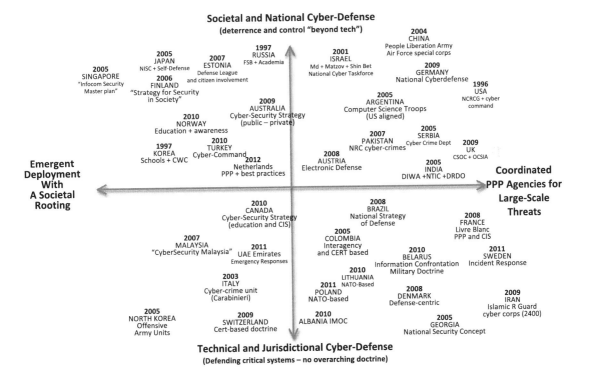

Figure 7

Erasing traces of presence, or traces of intrusion, has been long mastered by the hacking community, leading to the conclusion that diplomatic efforts are geared toward resolving an issue that has lost its technological pertinence before 2007.

Understanding the social psychology of threats development is becoming critical, as we are entering a pioneering period that strangely resembles the "phreaking" years of hacking (1972–1987). The improved portability of machine learning (embarked, distributed, or fully autonomous) is curiously absent from most national strategies' assumptions. This may be driven by the transposition of the principles of military capabilities escalation (weapons race, concentration, and decisive capacities) to the tackling of cyber-criminality. Cybernetic offensive capabilities do not respond to traditional escalation and reinforcement models. They derive their malevolent capabilities from their transformational nature, their distributed deployment, and their superior and autonomous learning.

References

Barreno, M., P.L. Bartlett, F.J. Chi, A.D. Joseph, B. Nelson, B.I.P. Rubinstein, U. Saini, and J.D. Tygar. 2008. "Open Problems in the Security of Learning", *First ACM Workshop on Security and Artificial Intelligence* (AISec), , Alexandria, Virginia, 19-26

Baumard, P. 1994. "From Information Warfare to Knowledge Warfare." In *Information Warfare*, ed. W. Schwartau. New York: Thunder's Mouth Press, 611-626

Bodmer, Kilger, Carpenter, and Jones. 2012. *Reverse Deception: Organized Cyber Threat Counter-Exploitation*. New York: McGraw-Hill Osborne Media.

Gaycken, S. 2012. "Die sieben Plagen des Cyberwar." In *Automatisierung und Digitalisierung des Krieges*, eds. R. Schmidt-Radefeldt, and C. Meissler. Berlin: Forum Innere Führung.

Rubinstein, B. I.P., B.Nelson, L. Huang, A.D. Joseph, S.-H. Lau, S. Rao, N. Taft, and J.D. Tygar. 2009. *"ANTIDOTE: Understanding and Defending against Poisoning of Anomaly Detectors", IMC '09: Proceedings of the Ninth ACM SIGCOMM on Internet Measurement Conference*, Chicago, IL, 1-14.

Sterling, B. 1994. *"Part Three: Law and Order". The Hacker Crackdown: Law And Disorder On The Electronic Frontier*. New York: Bantam Books.

Stoll, C. 1988. "Stalking the Wily Hacker." *Communications of the ACM* 31 (5): 484-500.

Stoll, C. 1989. *The Cuckoo's Egg: Tracking a Spy Through the Maze of Computer Espionage*. New-York: DoubleBay.

Criminal State and Illicit Economy: a Game Changer for the Twenty-First Century: Crime, Illicit Trades, Economy, and state

Mickaël Roudaut[A]

Introduction

Taking advantage of globalization, crime, and illicit trades grew to become, beyond *public security*[1], a question of *global and national security*[2] influencing international relations, economy, and society as a whole. Moreover, the classic divide between state and organized crime, the former fighting the latter, is no longer the single rule of the game.

Nowadays, in various countries and areas within them, organized crime and state interests can be found hard to distinguish to the point that the state may no longer seek to eradicate or reduce the organized crime pressure but may aim to control trafficking rings for its economic, personal, and partners benefits.

Furthermore, the millions of employees of the illicit economy producing counterfeits, smuggling hundreds of thousands of migrants, harvesting coca leaves or scratching poppy fields, poaching elephant or tiger carcasses, and pursuing the laundering of the proceeds in the licit economy on the one side and the millions more buying contraband cigarettes, smoking cannabis, paying for sex from coerced women, or employing irregular migrants on the other, create a vast global market. Given its scale and profitability, this illicit economy became a suppletive and at times an alternative model of development, closely intertwined with the legal sphere.

Yet, such awareness tends to remain confined to a few academic spheres instead of being fully acknowledged within international relations, political economy, and geopolitics so as to be translated at policy making level.

[A] Author of *Marchés criminels—Un acteur global* (2010), Presses Universitaires de France, Paris. Lecturer at the Universities of Paris II Panthéon-Assas, Clermont-Ferrand and at the *Gendarmerie nationale* Officers academy.

[1] To public, property, and business.

[2] To sovereignty, government, and economic and global stability.

[3] Geocriminology (neologism from the author) studies the rivalries of power within a given territory in its political, social, economic, geographic, and perceived dimensions (i.e., the emotional and spiritual dimension of a territory forging the Nation and by extension what is rightfully "mine" e.g., Los Angeles gang outbursts and Mexican cartels confrontation) through interactions between illicit flows, their actors, and the legal sphere. It also covers the use of illicit means by legal actors. These actions, inherently illegal but considered legitimate, are covered by the reason of state. Mickaël R. Roudaut, "Marchés criminels—un acteur global", PUF, coll. Questions judiciaires, May 2010, 304p, "Géopolitique de l'illicite", Diplomatie no. 50, May–June 2011, "Géopolitique de la crise, des monnaies et de la fraude", Diplomatie no. 55, March–April 2012, "Géopolitique de l'illicite : une nouvelle grammaire", in Géographie des conflits (Dir. Béatrice Giblin), La Documentation française, May 2012, "In Narco Veritas? Géocriminologie du Mexique et de sa région. Marchés criminels, économie et État", Sécurité Globale no. 21, automn 2012, "Sécurité intérieure et crime organisé au XXIe siècle: un essai de typologie" in Sécurité intérieure—Les nouveaux défis (Dir. Frédéric Debove & Olivier Renaudie), June 2013, "La multiplication et la diversification des acteurs illicites" in Questions internationales no. 63, September–October 2013, "Kaboul–Paris: voyage d'un gramme d'héroïne—Pouvoir et puissance de l'économie du pavot", Géoéconomie no. 68, January 2014.

That is why the traditional notions of organized crime, corruption, and penetration of public bodies no longer suffice to fully embrace and understand the modern relations between crime, illicit trades, economy, and state. Geocriminology[3], the geopolitics of illicit economy, aims to expose this reality and its impacts.

Crime is Shaping the World

Since the end of the Cold War, an unprecedented openness in trade, travel, communication, and finance has created an equally unprecedented era of economic growth and technological innovation, for the benefit of both citizens and consumers. Yet, as global governance struggles to keep pace with this destruction of barriers, massive criminal opportunities have emerged that exploit the open market economy.

Indeed, transnational organized crime changed in five defining ways:

1. From a mono-activity centered on drug trafficking, it expanded its reach investing in various illicit trades (counterfeiting, cigarettes, or migrants) and smuggling of all kinds once the routes and logistics are in place and in white-collar crimes.

2. From a centralized and vertical model, criminal groups evolved into amorphous, loose, adaptable, and flat transnational networks. Should a cell or some members be identified and arrested, the overall network would reconfigure itself almost naturally.

3. Criminal groups, turned illicit entrepreneurs, refined their *modi operandi* from expertise in passing borders to penetration of the licit economy through gained stakes and influence over strategic markets[4] (natural resources, energy, waste, and financial sector) while taking advantage of new technologies to access information, conceal their identity, and reduce detection risk.

4. The long-time barrier between organized crime and terrorism fell. Nowadays, a blend of insurgency, crime, and terrorism is at play whether in Sahel, the Af-Pak border, or in the longstanding example of the Andean forests (FARC[5], ELN[6], and *Sendero luminoso*[7]). Many terrorist groups, no longer or less state sponsored while in need of sustainable and discreet source of income, turned to illicit trades (notably counterfeiting, cigarette, and drugs). Hezbollah[8], Abu Sayyaf Group, Al Qaeda's Affiliates such as Al-Qaeda in Islamic Maghreb or

---

[4] See *Infra*.

[5] *Fuerzas Armadas Revolucionarias de Colombia*/Revolutionary Armed Forces of Colombia.

[6] *Ejército de Liberación Nacional*/National Liberation Army.

[7] Shining Path.

[8] In March 2006, the U.S. Federal Bureau of Investigation (FBI) busted a global network of counterfeit medicine fuelling Hezbollah with branches stretching from Brazil to China through Canada and Lebanon. More recently, for the U.S. Treasury Department, the "*Lebanese Canadian Bank—through management complicity, failure of internal controls, and lack of application of prudent banking standards—has been used extensively by persons associated with an international drug trafficking and money laundering network to move hundreds of millions of dollars monthly in cash proceeds…—as much as $200 million per month—… from illicit drug sales into the formal financial system*". "*According to U.S. Government information, Hizballah derived financial support from the criminal activities of Joumaa's network. LCB managers are also linked to Hizballah officials outside of Lebanon*". Press release, February 10, 2011.

Haqqani Network, PKK[9], Hamas, Islamic Jihad, terrorist movements in Northern Ireland, Kosovo, or Chechen separatists to name a few, have been or are considered engaged in organized crime-type activities[10]. This crime-terror nexus does not limit itself to terrorism turning to organized crime but also concerns the adoption of terror tactics by criminals. The filming of executions, amputations, decapitations, and hangings by Mexican criminal groups corresponds to the well-known strategy of tension aiming to attract Mexico into the cycle of repression-vengeance, with the prospects of police blunders (extra-judicial killings), that would undermine the legitimacy of the state[11]. Violence is therefore political. The D-Company, a criminal organization first invested in smuggling activities (1970s), evolved into a fully fledged organized crime group also engaged in insurgency-terrorism through "*supporting efforts to smuggle weapons to militant and terrorist groups*". "*By the 1990s, it began to conduct and participate in terrorist attacks, including the March 12, 1993, Bombay bombing*"[12].

5. In various countries and regions within them, crime and state seem to have, at least partially, merged, giving rise to a new type of organized crime entity, the criminal state.

Every year, hundreds of billions of dollars are produced by illicit trades and are essentially laundered in the licit economy[13], dozens of conflicts are fuelled by the smuggling of small arms and light weapons. Digital piracy (partially organized crime related), in less than a decade, transformed the movie and music industries and on average, 10,000 to 20,000 opioid users die each year from overdose, drug-related infectious diseases, violence, and other causes in the EU, Norway, and Turkey combined[14]. This influence on society, by all accounts, is found more lasting than any terrorist attacks.

Of course, criminal groups rip the benefits from these illicit trades to finance necessary workforce and protection from lawful authorities (corruption), to the point of competing with states in both "monopol[ies] of the legitimate violence" (Weber)[15] and taxation (through extortion).

Evolution of Transnational Organized Crime and National Security Implications

This contributes to the burgeoning of so-called "failed states", or more eloquently said, sovereigns without power, along major illicit trade routes. The global and local impacts of the illicit economy, from the Andean forest to French suburbs and North America through West Africa and

---

[9] *Partiya Karkerên Kurdistan*/Kurdistan Workers' Party.
[10] European Parliament, *Europe's Crime-terror Nexus: Links between Terrorist and Organised Crime Groups in the European Union*, 2012, 65 and CRS, *Terrorism and Transnational Crime: Foreign Policy Issues for Congress*, October 19, 2012, 40.
[11] Mickaël R. Roudaut, In *Narco Veritas?*, Op. cit.
[12] CRS, *Terrorism and Transnational Crime*, Op. cit.
[13] According to the UNODC (United Nations Office on Drugs and Crime), criminals, especially drug traffickers, may have laundered around US$1.6 trillion, or 2.7% of global GDP, in 2009. See *Infra*.
[14] EMCDDA (European Monitoring Centre for Drugs and Drug Addiction), European Drug Report 2013, May 2013, spec. p. 42.
[15] For a case study, see Mickaël R. Roudaut, In Narco Veritas? Op. cit.

Evolution of Transnational Organized Crime and National Security Implications

To view images, scan codes with phone,
or visit http://pso.site50.net/Roudaut_Figure_1A.png
and http://pso.site50.net/Roudaut_Figure_1B.png

Source: U.S. Office of the Director of National Intelligence, *The threat to U.S. national security posed by transnational organized crime*, 2011

Central America, leave no country immune.

Indeed, this pervasiveness concerns developed countries as well. After all, among the 10 generally acknowledged mafia-type organizations, seven find their origins in G8 countries[16].

Beyond, the intertwinement of state and crime concerns countries stranded on corruption reefs, hostages of the narco-economy or in the midst of political turmoil, or all of the above united in a perfect storm (Afghanistan and Guinea-Bissau)[17].

"It is impossible to understand all the workings that govern prices, intermediaries or the structure of supply networks of Russian gas that arrives in Europe (transiting notably by Ukraine) without taking into account the role of organized crime"[18].

As an illustration of this quantum leap from public security to global and national security concerns, an alleged criminal, present on the FBI 10 most wanted fugitives list for being suspected of having defrauded investors of more than 150 million dollars from 1993 to 1998 is also and more importantly reputed to be involved in the Eastern European gas market.

According to the FBI and the Department of Justice, he "*uses his ill-gotten gains to influence governments and their economies*"[19].

In a meeting with the U.S. Ambassador in Kiev, reported in a 2008 diplomatic cable released by WikiLeaks, the nominal owner of the company distributing gas to the EU allegedly "*acknowledged ties to [the] Russian organized crime figure [identified hereabove], stating he needed [his] approval to get into business in the first place [...]. He noted that it was impossible to approach a government official for any reason without also meeting with an organized crime member at the same time. [He] acknowledged that he needed, and received, permission from [this Russian organized crime figure] when he established various businesses, but he denied any close relationship to him. If he needed a permit from the government, for example, he would invariably need permission from the appropriate 'businessman' who worked with the government official who issued the particular permit. He maintained that the era of the 'law of the street' had passed and businesses could now be run legitimately in Ukraine*"[20].

---

[16] Cosa Nostra, Camorra, 'Ndrangheta, Sacra Corona Unita, and Stidda in Italy, U.S. Cosa Nostra, and Yakuza in Japan. The three remaining being the Triads in China, the Turkish maffya and the Albanian-speaking mafia while a scholar debate takes place concerning vory v zakone (a part of Russian organized crime) regarding its mafia status. A mafia can be defined as a secret society or an institutionalized association anchored in a territory while having an international and polycriminal activity. Readily compartmentalized and hierarchical even though a looser network of cells can also be used, a genuine mafia is driven by a set of rites (including initiation), rules (omerta …), and beliefs. Its recruitment is usually based on family and clan. Should all these criteria be met, only the test of time can confer the mafia qualification, hence the debate over vory v zakone. For an example of Mafia code of honor see the Triads 36 commitments oath, Thierry Cretin, *Mafia* (s) (Chronique editions, 2009),124–5.

[17] M. Naím, "La mafia au cœur de l'État", Slate, May 10, 2012.

[18] Unofficial translation, Idem.

[19] FBI, "Global Con Artist" Attorney General Michael B. Mukasey, "Attorney General Michael B. Mukasey Delivers Remarks at the CSIS Forum on Combating International Organized Crime", April 23, 2008, *Political/Congressional Transcript Wire in CRS, Organized Crime: An Evolving Challenge for U.S. Law Enforcement*, January 6, 2012.

[20] Cable #002414, December 10, 2008, http://www.guardian.co.uk/world/us-embassy-cables-documents/182121 and cable #002294, November 21, 2008 http://www.guardian.co.uk/world/us-embassy-cables-documents/179510

Perhaps logically, the 2011 U.S. Strategy to combat transnational organized crime (TOC) considers TOC, a novelty, as a "*national security threat*" while urging other states to undertake a similar step[21].

The U.S. President goes on to declare, "*Criminal networks are not only expanding their operations, but they are also diversifying their activities, resulting in a convergence of transnational threats that has evolved to become more complex, volatile, and destabilizing. These networks also threaten U.S. interests by forging alliances with corrupt elements of national governments and using the power and influence of those elements to further their criminal activities. In some cases, national governments exploit these relationships to further their interests to the detriment of the United States*"[22].

This last sentence, a rare instance in official publications, underlines the following; governments can, for reason of state or less legitimate motives, protect, take advantage of, or control and develop criminal activities. This further reveals the geopolitical nature of crime and its systemic impact. It notably justifies the shift from public to global and national security concerns.

However, the traditional legal and operational toolbox made of treaties, international, regional, and bilateral cooperation and dedicated organizations appears ill-adapted to this new type of criminal player proven as flexible and agile as organized crime while enjoying the legal privileges and immunities of states[23].

The Inbreeding of Organized Crime and State: From Reason of State to Criminal State

The defining trait of the twenty-first century, as mentioned in Obama's statement, organized crime can be overtaken by states, not as to be destroyed, but as to be controlled in view to reap the benefit of its illicit deeds.

As any living creature, a state is driven by one paramount instinct; survive and thrive. History shows that no action will be spared to ensure this very survival, including, of course, through actions that would be deemed illegal if not covered by the reason of state. If history has found legitimacy in some of them, nowadays, illegal state actions involving organized crime no longer seem to be directly led by this survival imperium but rather more economic and prosaic personal wealth. A symbiotic relation between state and crime is thus developed[24].

Bulgaria

Another quantum leap example from public security to global and national security concerns can be found in a now aged 2005 U.S. diplomatic cable released by WikiLeaks. "*TIM [described as a major organized crime group] controls some of the largest quarries of inert materials in Bulgaria, and through its trading company [...] it also has a significant share of the production and trade in fertilizers, petroleum products, and chemicals*"[25].

---

[21] Following on the 2010 National Intelligence Estimate on international organized crime which first in the United States made the shift from public security threat to national security threat.
[22] White House, *U.S. Strategy to Combat Transnational Organized Crime*, June 2011, iii.
[23] M. Naím, *opus citum*.
[24] Mickaël R. Roudaut, *Sécurité intérieure et crime organisé au XXIe siècle*, Op. cit.
[25] Cable #001207, July 7, 2005, http://wikileaks.ch/cable/2005/07/05SOFIA1207.html

For the author of the cable "Organized crime has a corrupting influence on all Bulgarian institutions, including the government, parliament and judiciary. In an attempt to maintain their influence regardless of who is in power, OC [Organized Crime] figures donate to all the major political parties. As these figures have expanded into legitimate businesses, they have attempted—with some success—to buy their way into the corridors of power. [...] Below the level of the national government and the leadership of the major political parties, OC "owns" a number of municipalities and individual members of parliament. This direct participation in politics—as opposed to bribery—is a relatively new development for Bulgarian OC. At the municipal level, a by-election earlier this year in the town of [...] resulted in the complete takeover of the municipal government by figures who have made little attempt to conceal their links to powerful smuggling interests. Similarly in the regional center of [...], OC figures control the municipal council and the mayor's office. Nearly identical scenarios have played out in half a dozen smaller towns and villages across Bulgaria"[26].

Italy

Crime and politics in Italy have been extensively reported and studied. The aim is not to remind us of well-known corruption and influence cases but whether *pacta sceleris* reached a level of national security concern.

A key point, notably developed by Umberto Santino, states that Italian mafias are not always against the state since "*they are 'in' and 'with' the state as well*"[27] through the "mafia bourgeoisie". "Criminal groups, a few thousand members in total, interact with a much larger social group within which decision-making power is exercised by illegal actors [...] and by legal actors, professionals, entrepreneurs, public servants, elected politicians and officials in charge of institutions, [forming] a mafia bourgeoisie"[28].

Camorra (6,700), 'Ndrangheta (6,000), Cosa Nostra (5,200), Sacra Corona Unita (1,800), and Stidda (unknown), represent roughly "only" 20,000 persons. Their impact cannot be understood without this necessary interaction with the "mafia bourgeoisie"[29].

This interaction was illustrated again in a recent police operation in Calabria, the birthplace of the 'Ndrangheta. Arrest warrants were issued against 65 people in Lamezia Terme, in the area of Catanzaro; among them, "*entrepreneurs, politicians and lawyers as well as doctors and staff of the prison administration*"[30].

Criminal powers anchored in a territory (mafias and cartels) possess an electoral power (votes). In 2004, 190 "families" were identified (approximately 5,200 members) in Sicily, among which 89 were in the province of Palermo (about 3,200 members)[31]. On average, each "man of honor" controlling 40 to 50 votes, the electoral base of the Cosa Nostra in the Palermo prov-

---

[26] Idem.

[27] Arles Arloff, "Italie, un pouvoir corrompu," *Futuribles* no. 381, January 2012.

[28] Umberto Santino, *La mafia interpretata Dilemmi, Stereotipi, paradigmi* (Rubbettino editions, 1995), 250, p. 145 in Arles Arloff and André-Yves Portnoff, "La mafia italienne : persistances et résistance", *Futuribles* no. 326, January 2007, 32.

[29] T. Cretin, *Mafia(s)*, Op. cit., p. 21, 25, 31, 36, and 38–39.

[30] *Le Monde*, "Italie: opérations anti-mafia d'ampleur menées à Rome et en Calabre", July 26, 2013.

[31] T. Cretin, *Mafia(s)*, Op. cit., 21.

ince would range from 128,000 to 160,000 votes[32], enough to mediate the political debate, or even hold its key.

For the anti-mafia deputy prosecutor of Calabria, "*the 'Ndrangheta [...] controls 20% of votes, it is sufficient to switch the majorities in our small towns*"[33].

Criminal powers are thus both fought and courted by law abiding personnel and corruptible individuals. Unsurprisingly, from July 1991 to February 2008, 172 municipal councils were dissolved for operating under mafia influence[34].

The trial for "*participation in a criminal association*" of a key figure, from the years 1955 to 1992, seven times President of the Council (Prime Minister), Andreotti, leave limited room for speculation on the national security concern reached by organized crime penetration in Italy. The supreme court in its October 2004 ruling declared that "*during the 1970s and through to the spring of 1980, Andreotti enjoyed friendly and direct relations with leading members of Cosa Nostra and had knowingly and deliberately cultivated a stable relationship with Mafiosi. [...] The judgment found that Andreotti had been involved in criminal association until spring of 1980, but the crime was time-barred and insufficient proof brought him acquittal for the time after that*"[35]. In other words, Andreotti was found guilty of criminal association but the expiry of the statute of limitation prevented any sentence. The ruling was translated by the Italian press in a simple acquittal.

For the U.S. Department of State, "*The proceeds of domestic organized crime groups (especially the Camorra, the 'Ndrangheta, and the Mafia) operating across numerous economic sectors in Italy and abroad compose the main source of laundered funds. Numerous reports by Italian non-governmental organizations identify domestic organized crime as Italy's largest enterprise*"[36].

Japan

The Japanese situation can be difficult to apprehend for western eyes. To the opposite of criminal wisdom, *yakuza* (or *boryokudan*) possess clearly identified offices, give away business cards, may grant interviews, and are the subject of fan magazines. They can compete with traditional companies in the hiring of graduates straight out of business schools. The relation between state, power, and *yakuza* is thus well documented[37].

Comprising roughly 79,000 persons divided among 22 groups (in 2012), they are considered to have played a key role in the decade long recession that hit Japan at the beginning of the 1990s, to the point that the period is often referred to as the "*yakuza recession*"[38].

---

[32] According to the *pentito* Antonino Calderone (1987) and Xavier Raufer (http://www.xavier-raufer.com).

[33] *Le Monde*, November 7, 2005.

[34] Italian Parliament, *Relazione annuale della Commissione parlamentare di inchiesta sul fenomeno della criminalità organizzata mafiosa o similare 'ndrangheta'*, 2008, 116.

[35] David Lane, *Into the heart of the Mafia*, 2010 (Profile books LTD), 4.

[36] Department of State, *International Narcotics Control Strategy Report*, Vol. II, March 2013, 141.

[37] David Kapan and Alec Dubro, *Yakuza* (du Picquier editions, 2002), Thierry Cretin, *Mafia(s)*, Op. cit., 130–141, *Foreign Policy*, "The Yakuza lobby", December 13, 2012.

[38] *Far Eastern Economic Review*, The Yakuza Recession, January 17, 2002: "*Neither Miyawaki nor any other credible commentator suggests that deflation, policy blunders, political inertia and a whole range of other factors haven't contributed to Japan's decade-long stagnation. All the same, Miyawaki, a Tokyo University Law School graduate, former spokesman for Prime Minister Yasuhiro Nakasone and former head of the National Police*

To view images, scan codes with phone,
or visit http://pso.site50.net/Roudaut_Figure_2.png

Source: Japan National Police Academy, Police Policy Research Center, *Crime in Japan* in 2009

As illustration of the global and national security concern *yakuza* represent, a 2007 Japan police report warned that "*the yakuza made such incursions into the financial market that they threaten the very basis of the Japanese economy*"[39]. More recently, they "*have been tied to a wide range of businesses, including the nuclear industry*[40] *and [...] a Japanese camera manufacturer mired in a major accounting scandal*"[41].

As another illustration of the global reach of the *yakuza*, following the Executive Order, issued in 2011 by President Obama to target and disrupt four major transnational criminal organizations (Brother's circle, Eurasian based—Camorra, Italian based—Yakuza and Zetas, Mexican based)[42], the U.S. Treasury announced in February 2012 the freezing of the American-based assets of the *Yamaguchi-gumi*, the larger *yakuza* group, and two of its leaders. It will also bar any transactions between Americans and members of this crime syndicate.

Shaping their image, a longstanding feature of mafia-type organizations, the *yakuza* "*were some of the first responders after the earthquake [that provoked the tsunami hitting the Fukushima power plant], providing food and supplies to the devastated area and patrolling the streets to make sure no looting occurred*"[43].

Kosovo

In 2011, the Parliamentary Assembly of the Council of Europe adopted a widely commented report investigating organ trafficking in Kosovo. It held the view that "*[...] in confidential reports spanning more than a decade, agencies dedicated to combating drug smuggling in at least five countries have named Hashim Thaqi [Prime Minister of Kosovo] and other members of his 'Drenica Group' as having exerted violent control over the trade in heroin and other narcotics*"[44].

"*In the course of the last ten years, intelligence services from several Western European countries, law enforcement agencies, including the Federal Bureau of Investigation (FBI) in the United States, and analysts of several nationalities working within NATO structures have prepared authoritative, well-sourced, corroborated reports on the unlawful activities of this 'Drenica Group'*"[45].

"*At a minimum, there is solid documentary evidence to demonstrate the involvement of this group, and its financial sponsors, in money laundering, smuggling of drugs and cigarettes, human trafficking, prostitution, and the violent monopolisation of Kosovo's largest economic sectors including vehicle fuel and construction*"[46].

[38 (cont)] *Agency's organized crime division, estimates that up to 50% of the bad debts held by Japanese banks could be impossible to recover because they involve organized crime and corrupt politicians*", thus slowing down the decade long recovery process, hence the "yakuza recession" moniker.

[39] *Foreign policy*, "The Yakuza lobby", Op. cit.

[40] *The Telegraph*, "How the Yakuza went nuclear", February 21, 2012.

[41] *New York Times*, "U.S. Treasury Dept. Penalizes Japan's Largest Organized-Crime Group", February 24, 2012.

[42] Executive order #13581, July 24, 2011.

[43] *The Telegraph*, Op. cit.

[44] Council of Europe, Parliamentary Assembly, Report #12462, *Inhuman treatment of people and illicit trafficking in human organs in Kosovo*, January 2011. Paragraph 66 and footnote 28: The agencies dedicated to combatting drug smuggling are "*the German (BND), Italian (Sismi), British (MI6) and Greek (EYP) intelligence services*".

[45] Ibidem, footnote 31.

Myanmar

Viewed from Bangkok press, "Among the candidates who won in the South-east Asian nation's first election in 20 years on Nov. 7 [2010] are six well-known drug barons. They represented the Union Solidarity and Development Party, the junta's political front, which triumphed comfortably in the poll"[47].

For the U.S. Department of State "[Birman] policy of folding ethnic armed groups into quasi [state]-controlled [border guard forces—BGFs] complicates anti-narcotics efforts as BGFs are often complicit, if not active protectors, of illicit drug production and trafficking. [...]. [...] [Government] officials are likely aware of the cultivation, production, and trafficking of illegal narcotics in areas they control"[48].

"Many inside Burma assume some senior government officials benefit financially from narcotics trafficking, but these assumptions have never been confirmed through arrests, convictions, or other public revelations. Credible reports from NGOs and media claim that mid-level military officers and government officials were engaged in drug-related corruption; however, no military officer above the rank of colonel has ever been charged with drug-related corruption"[49].

"The Burmese government considers drug enforcement secondary to national stability and is willing to allow narcotics trafficking in border areas in exchange for cooperation from ethnic armed groups and militias"[50].

"Political arrangements between traffickers and Burma's government allow organized crime groups to function with minimal risk of interdiction"[51].

Nicaragua

According to two 2006 U.S. diplomatic cables released by WikiLeaks, organized crime and state seemed to have followed a partnership pattern.

"In 1984 Daniel Ortega [at power from 1979 to 1985, Head of state from 1985 to 1990 and since 2007] negotiated a deal with Colombian drug kingpin Pablo Escobar whereby Escobar received refuge for several months in Nicaragua after he had ordered the killing of the Colombian Minister of Justice. At the same time, Escobar's drug trafficking operation received Ortega's approval to land and load airplanes in Nicaragua as they sought to ship cocaine to the United States. In return, Ortega and the FSLN [Sandinista National Liberation Front] received large cash payments from Escobar. [The] Interior Minister [...] and his subordinates went so far as to assist Escobar with the loading and unloading of drugs onto his airplanes in Nicaragua. The Drug Enforcement Agency (DEA) managed to place a hidden camera on one of Escobar's airplanes and obtained film of Escobar and Ministry of the Interior officials loading cocaine onto one of Escobar's planes at Managua's international airport. CBS news later broadcast the film"[52].

"Daniel Ortega and the Sandinista have regularly received money to finance FSLN electoral campaigns from international

---

[46] Ibid., footnote 32.

[47] *IPS*, "Junta's Drug Exports to China test Economic Ties", December 31, 2010.

[48] Department of State, *International Narcotics Control Strategy Report*, Vol. I, March 2012, 144-147.

[49] Department of State, *International Narcotics Control Strategy Report*, Vol. I, March 2013, 114.

[50] Ibid., 112.

[51] Department of State, *International Narcotics Control Strategy Report*, Vol. II, March 2013, 77.

[52] Cable #63026, May 5, 2006. http://www.elpais.com/articulo/internacional/Cable/delitos/abusos/regimen/Daniel/Ortega/elpepuint/20101206elpepuint_35/Tes

drug traffickers, usually in return for ordering Sandinista judges to allow traffickers caught by the police and military to go free"⁵³.

As for the neighboring Panamá, his former leader and CIA informant, Manuel Noriega, ousted by the United States in 1989 was first condemned for drug trafficking and money laundering and sentenced to 30 years imprisonment in Florida, reduced to 17 for "good behavior". Extradited to France, he was condemned to a seven years jail sentence for money laundering. He was extradited to Panamá in December 2011.

North Korea

Pyongyang has notably been accused by the U.S. government of counterfeiting its currency *"apparently done to generate foreign exchange that is used to purchase imports or finance government activities abroad"*⁵⁴.

Russia

In a 2010 widely reported U.S. diplomatic cable released by WikiLeaks, a senior Spanish prosecutor investigating organized crime *"gave a detailed, frank assessment of the activities and reach of organized crime (OC) in both Eurasia and Spain"*. For [Belarus, Chechnya and Russia] he alleged, one cannot differentiate between the activities of the government and OC groups". For him, Russian organized crime *"exercises 'tremendous control' over certain strategic sectors of the global economy, such as aluminum"*⁵⁵.

*"[He] said that according to information he has received from intelligence services, witnesses and phone taps, certain political parties in Russia operate 'hand in hand' with OC. For example, he argued that the Liberal Democratic Party (LDP) was created by the KGB and its successor, the SVR, and is home to many serious criminals. [He] further alleged that there are proven ties between the Russian political parties, organized crime and arms trafficking. Without elaborating, he cited the strange case of the 'Artic Sea' ship in mid-2009 as 'a clear example' of arms trafficking"*⁵⁶.

*"He summarized his views by asserting that the [Moscow]'s strategy is to use OC groups to do whatever [it] cannot acceptably do as a government. As an example, he cited [an individual arrested in Spain], whom he said worked for Russian military intelligence to sell weapons to the Kurds to destabilize Turkey. [The Spanish prosecutor] claimed that [Moscow] takes the relationship with OC leaders even further by granting them the privileges of politics, in order to grant them immunity from racketeering charges"*⁵⁷.

*"[The Spanish prosecutor] said that he believes the FSB is 'absorbing' the Russian mafia but they can also 'eliminate' them in two ways: by killing OC leaders who do not do what the security services want them to do or by putting them behind bars to eliminate them as a competitor for influence. The crime lords can also be put in jail for their own protection"*⁵⁸.

---

⁵³ Cable #63040, May 5, 2006. http://www.elpais.com/articulo/internacional/Cable/jueces/sandinistas/ponen/libertad/narcos/cambio/dinero/elpepuesp/20101206elpepuint_37/Tes

⁵⁴ CRS, *North Korean Counterfeiting of U.S. Currency*, June 12, 2009, 15 p. and 22 mars 2006, 18 p., *International Herald Tribune*, August 20, 2006 "North Korea linked to Asian Banks", *Foreign Policy*, September–October 2008, 61.

⁵⁵ Cable #000154, February 8, 2010 http://www.guardian.co.uk/world/us-embassy-cables-documents/247712.

⁵⁶ *Id.*

⁵⁷ *Id.*

⁵⁸ *Id.*

Transnational Organized Crime: Examples of a Diverse and Global Threat

To view images, scan codes with phone,
or visit http://pso.site50.net/Roudaut_Figure_3.png

Source: U.S. Office of the Director of National Intelligence, *The threat to U.S. national security posed by transnational organized crime*, 2011

Beyond the international reaction triggered by the death of Sergueï Magnitsky, the case, 230 million dollars seemingly defrauded, allegedly with the complicity of several officials in relations with Russian organized crime, would seem, if confirmed, to embody what the Spanish prosecutor described.

The Illicit Economy: A Suppletive and Alternative Model of Development

A fact often misunderstood when it is simply considered, organized crime and illicit markets, just as the Cold War in the twentieth century and colonization in the nineteenth, grew to become a new geopolitical framework of the twenty-first century. They influence the evolution of society both at global and local levels as surely as the decisions taken within the G20, the World Trade Organization (WTO), or the International Monetary Fund (IMF)[59]. They also fuel a double phenomenon of politicization of crime and criminalization of politics[60].

That is why beyond traditional divides between North and South, developed, emerging, and least developed economies, a paradigm shift is probably at play whereby 'functional' states, and areas within them, are found able to limit the criminal influence below the limit of what can be deemed acceptable and the others, where organized crime and illicit trades represent both a suppletive and alternative model of development.

A consequence of the Social Pact, transition from Behemoth to Leviathan (Hobbes), the legitimacy of state derives from its ability to provide security, employment, and reasonable prospects in climbing the social ladder. When failing to do so, the vacuum is often filled, in various areas of the world, including of course within developed countries, by criminal actors. In the end the state loses its legitimacy. This is the demise of the Social Pact.

The illicit economy, held up as a suppletive and alternative model of development, corrodes the licit sphere through corruption and the laundering of proceeds of crime. Thus, organized crime and illicit markets embody a new "invisible hand"[61]. And that is precisely the point if one wants to truly grasp the dynamic between licit and illicit economy nowadays. It is impossible to understand the effect of counterfeiting without considering the importance of this industry for some regions and states. It is impossible to shed light on small arms and light weapons trafficking without considering the role played by its intermediaries, small players in a greater cause (reason of state). It is impossible to understand the complexity of irregular migration without considering that for some economies the money sent back home, in hard currencies, from the migrants "lucky" enough to land themselves an undeclared work in Europe or North America can represent an essential part of the national GDP, thus contributing to prevention of social unrest. It is impossible again to grasp the issue of grand corruption, tax evasion, and money

---

[59] Mickaël R. Roudaut, *Marchés criminels—Un acteur global*, Op. cit.

[60] M. Naím, "The Drug Trade: The Politicization of Criminals and the Criminalization of Politicians", *Global Commission on Drug Policies*, January 2011, 8.

[61] Mickaël R. Roudaut, *Géopolitique de l'illicite—la nouvelle main invisible*, Op. cit. and *Marchés criminels—Un acteur global*. "In economics, the invisible hand of the market is a metaphor to describe the self-regulating behavior of the marketplace. The idea of markets automatically channeling self-interest toward socially desirable ends

To view images, scan codes with phone,
or visit http://pso.site50.net/Roudaut_Figure_5.pdf

Source: Mickaël R. Roudaut, "Géopolitique de l'illicite: une nouvelle grammaire", *Géographie des conflits (Dir. Béatrice Giblin)*, La Documentation française, March 2012

laundering without recognizing the central role played by financial opacity in the global economy..."[62]

Beyond, this illicit and criminal force challenges the very foundation of modern states, based on sovereignty, since, whatever the actors or techniques, organized crime and the illicit trades they operate are transnational. Not only borders became more difficult to control due to the explosion of commercial flows but crossing them represent a great profit incentive to criminals.

Two figures in this regard. "*The value of the drugs doubles with every border crossed: a gram of heroin worth $3 in Kabul may reach $100 on the streets of London, Milan or Moscow*"[63]. One kilo of sildenafil citrate, the active ingredient of Viagra, only costs 60 dollars in South Asia, diluted in thousands of tablets, this modest investment can be worth 300,000[64].

Thus, as an illustration of the polycriminal nature of transnational organized crime, "*a line of cocaine snorted in Europe kills one square meter of Andean rain forest and buys one hundred rounds of AK 47 ammunition in West Africa*"[65].

Geopolitics and Geoeconomics of Illicit and Criminal Markets

Geoeconomics of Drugs

The geoeconomics of drugs is well known. "*The overall value of the illicit drug market was estimated at about $320 billion for the year 2003, equivalent to 0.9 per cent of global GDP*"[66].

Of course, the heroin trade partly fuels both insurgency and terror. In total, the Taliban's income from the opiate trade in 2009 was around $155 million (ranging from 140 to 170)[67]. Beyond, "*UNODC estimates suggest that the value of Afghan traders' opiate-related sales was equivalent to slightly more than 60 per cent of the country's GDP in 2004. While this proportion decreased to 16 per cent in 2011, this figure is still very significant*"[68]. In other words, the opium trade would be worth an equivalent of one sixth of the Afghan "wealth".

Moreover, beyond the opiate trade, "*the total corruption cost has increased by some 40 per cent over the last three years to reach $3.9 billion*". "*Nearly 30 per cent of Afghan citizens paid a bribe when requesting a service from individuals not employed in the public sector of Afghanistan in 2012, as opposed to the 50 per cent who paid bribes to public officials*"[69].

---

is a central justification for the laissez-faire economic philosophy. In this sense, the central disagreement between economic ideologies can be viewed as a disagreement about how powerful the 'invisible hand' is" (Wikipedia). Nowadays, organized crime, based on illicit trades economy, can play a social role thus embodies this invisible hand.

[62] Mickaël R. Roudaut, *Marchés criminels—Un acteur global*, Op. cit.

[63] UNODC, *Addiction, Crime and Insurgency—The Transnational Threat of Afghan Opium*, Press release p. 2, October 21, 2009.

[64] *Foreign Policy*, "The Deadly World of Fake Drugs", September–October 2008, 61.

[65] Antonio Maria Costa, then UNODC Executive Director, UN Press Release, February 24, 2010.

[66] UNODC, *World Drug Report 2012*, 60.

[67] UNODC, *The Global Afghan Opium Trade—A Threat Assessment*, July 2011, p. 30.

[68] UNODC, *World Drug Report 2012*, p. 67.

The invasive power of the narco-economy expands well beyond Afghan territory to follow the heroin roads. *"With a net profit of US$1.4 billion only from heroin trade, drug traffickers earned almost 31 per cent of the GDP of Tajikistan ($4.58 billion) and 33 per cent of the GDP of Kyrgyzstan*[70]. *"[These countries] are in a sense dependent on the illicit opiates industry"*[71].

Important point, *"[T]he value of the Afghan opiate trade in Europe (Russia excluded) is no less than 20 times the value of the opiate trade in Pakistan (US$ 1 billion). The economic power accruing to criminal organizations running trafficking operations to Europe via the Balkan or the Northern routes dwarfs insurgents' benefits in Afghanistan and/or Pakistan. As a whole, Europe's stability is not threatened by the opiate trade, but the very large revenues they extract from the drug trade have given these groups the means to achieve considerable influence in some countries along trafficking routes"*[72].

In other words, since primarily enriching, thus empowering, European and Turkish criminal groups, heroin trafficking could perhaps be considered a European as much as an Afghan issue[73].

A similar link between the illicit and criminal economy and its impact on the state, albeit to a lesser degree, is found concerning cannabis in Morocco. The role of the cannabis economy in the Rif Mountains is well known. Serving as a social net, it prevents social unrest, irregular migration to Europe, and Islamism, further highlighting its geopolitical influence[74].

The U.S. Department of State reports, *"UNODC estimates that the cannabis crop provides incomes for 800,000 people, and accounts for 3.1% of Morocco's agricultural GDP. Police corruption and tacit non-enforcement remains an issue in Morocco"*[75].

Of course, the impact of the cannabis economy expands along the trafficking routes in Europe. Rather than referring to global figures that the reader is familiar with, the findings of a 2007 report from the French drugs observatory, a public institution, deserve attention.

In France, the cannabis economy would represent 100,000 street dealers. On a monthly basis, a semi-wholesaler would earn up to 46,000 euro a month; the average salary of a manager of a company with over 2,000 employees. The first intermediate (supplier) would also benefit substantially from the cannabis economy with a monthly salary of up to 6,400 euro. The last two levels of resellers (street dealer) would only make a maximum of 800 euro per month (which could be considered as a "cannabis minimum wage" since the net minimum salary in France is roughly 1,000 euro a month)[76].

The scale of the cannabis economy in France was further confirmed in a report from the organized crime intelligence and analysis department of French police. *"[C]riminal organizations from sensitive*

---

[69] UNODC, *Corruption in Afghanistan*, Press Release, February 7, 2013.

[70] UNODC, *The Global Afghan Opium Trade*, Op. cit., 47.

[71] UNODC, *World Drug Report 2010*, 48.

[72] UNODC, *Addiction, Crime and Insurgency—The Transnational Threat of Afghan Opium*, 2009, 18.

[73] Mickaël R. Roudaut, "Kaboul-Paris : voyage d'un gramme d'héroïne—Pouvoir et puissance de l'économie du pavot", Op. cit.

[74] Alain Labrousse, *Géopolitique des drogues*, PUF, Que-sais-je? Third Edition, 2011, 38.

[75] Department of State, *International Narcotics Control Strategy Report*, Vol. I, March 2013, 240.

[76] Christian Ben Lakhdar, *Le trafic de cannabis en France*, OFDT, November 2007, 25.

suburbs, responsible for massive imports of Moroccan cannabis (worth over 1 billion euro for a consumption of 250 tons a year) and continuous illegal drugs flows remain the main source of the underground economy in France"[77].

This represents both the suppletive and at times alternative model of development previously mentioned.

Geoeconomics of Counterfeiting

Counterfeiting, an industry probably claiming millions of jobs worldwide, serves as a social net within states and territories where they are well rooted. Tackling it would mean providing another future to these employees of the illicit trade. That is why its geoeconomics impact, from China to Turkey, Argentina or Morocco, is generally underrated.

While the costs are difficult to quantify, and do not include non-monetary damage such as illness and death, the value of counterfeiting is estimated by the OECD to be around $250 billion a year[78]. This figure does not include domestically produced and consumed counterfeits nor digital piracy. If these were added, the total amount of counterfeiting worldwide could be several hundred billion dollars more[79]. In 2011, the value of the equivalent genuine products of the 114 million IPR infringing articles detained at the EU external border was estimated to be over 1.2 billion euros[80].

What is the socio-economic cost of counterfeiting in Europe? Despite many reports, they tend, like a school of fish, to copy one another. The most common estimates evaluate at 200,000 the number of jobs lost each year in the EU because of counterfeiting. In France, 30,000 jobs are supposedly at stake. These figures, persistently quoted, serve as a reference. Yet, apparently neither built on reliable statistical basis nor on any comparable data, they rather reveal the absence of a more rigorous assessment of the socioeconomic consequences of the counterfeiting industry[81].

The same strategic gap has been emphasized in the United States by the Government Accountability Office (GAO—U.S. Congress). Faced with the identical issue of quantification and comparability of data, it concludes that the socioeconomic impact of counterfeiting on U.S. soil cannot be scientifically evaluated for lack of reliable data[82].

Furthermore, the more diverse counterfeiting becomes, the more it concerns products of daily use. In a causal link, the more counterfeiting attempts to penetrate official channels of distribution, and the more we all are at potential risk of buying fakes in good faith. There lies the

---

[77] "l'activisme et les capacités d'adaptation des organisations criminelles issues des cités sensibles, responsables des importations massives de cannabis marocain (plus d'un milliard d'euros pour environ 250 tonnes de résine de cannabis consommées annuellement selon la Police judiciaire) et le déploiement continu des flux de stupéfiants, demeurent la principale source d'irrigation de l'économie souterraine en France", *Le Figaro*, October 22, 2012.

[78] OECD, *Magnitude of Counterfeiting and Piracy of Tangible Products: An Update*, November 2009, 6.

[79] *Id.*

[80] European Commission, *Report on EU Customs Enforcement of Intellectual Property Rights—Results at the EU Border—2011*, July 2012, 7.

[81] Mickaël R. Roudaut, "From Sweatshops to Organized Crime: The New Face of Counterfeiting", in *Criminal Enforcement of Intellectual Property* (Edward Elgar Publishing, 2012), 75–95.

[82] United States Government Accountability Office, *Observations on Efforts to Quantify the Economic Effects of Counterfeit and Pirated Goods*, April 2010, 37.

main stake of our times. If there are many examples of penetration of official channels of distribution[83], no study evaluating this reality has however been conducted so far, highlighting how unknown this illicit trade remains in spite of being on everyone's lips. The same gap concerns the extent of counterfeits produced and trafficked in Europe.

Geopolitics of Natural Resources

The superposition of a map of civil conflicts with the cartography of natural resources in Africa presents similarities. Similarity is not causality, however in Sierra Leone, Liberia, and the Democratic Republic of Congo or more precisely in the Great Lakes region, or in Nigeria, the plundering of natural resources and its smuggling have played or play an important and well documented role in the financing, so in the prolongation, of these conflicts.

This is particularly the case in the Democratic Republic of Congo, where conflicts, whether declared or latent, oppose no less than six factions. Since all parties are partially if not essentially funded through natural resources, outbreaks concentrate around them. Ultimately, plundering of natural resources and civil wars feed one another.

On the long run, by contagion, it destabilizes entire regions which in turn pushes people to flee. Some, choosing exile in Europe, employ the services of criminal networks since irregular migration to the EU is considered essentially facilitated to one degree or another by organized crime.

Once in Europe, many of them, when asylum is not granted, can become irregular workers on construction sites, sell counterfeit, others (mostly women) can be coerced into prostitution rings illustrating the symbiotic links between irregular migration, trafficking in persons, undeclared labor, and violations of intellectual property rights, all this also impacting on the legal economy[84].

Geoeconomics of Irregular Migration

The lack of political will sometimes deplored in Europe or North America from the emigration states in the fight against irregular migration networks exploiting their nationals could find its origin in the following.

Not only candidates to exile mainly consist of "left behind" within disfranchised communities who, in lack of emigration prospects, could fuel social unrest (food riots...) but turning a blind eye on these criminal rings allows emigration countries to benefit from a means of economic development through remittances provided to family members remaining behind. Some of these countries heavily depend on this hard currency flow sometimes representing up to 45% of their GDP[85]. Ultimately, they are simply subsidized by their migrants illustrating how irregular migration can be necessary to their viability.

This trend could be reinforced with the expected increase of the global population, to, medium hypothesis, 11 billion persons in 2100. The number of people living on the African continent is set to nearly quadruple by the end of the century. Nigeria, a country slightly smaller than Texas and Colorado combined, could surpass

---

[83] Mickaël R. Roudaut, *From Sweatshops to Organized Crime: The New Face of Counterfeiting*, Op. cit.

[84] Mickaël R. Roudaut, *Marchés criminels—Un acteur global*, Op. cit. and *Géopolitique de l'illicite—la nouvelle main invisible*, Op. cit.

[85] UNODC (from World Bank data), *The Globalization of Crime: A Transnational Organized Crime Threat Assessment*, 2010, figure 41, 56.

the United States as the world's third-most populous country by 2050. The size of its population may rival that of China by the end of the century[86].

Financial Opacity: The Bridge Between Licit and Illicit Economies

Illicit trades are big business. The UNODC suggests that all criminal proceeds, excluding tax evasion, would have amounted to some 2.1 trillion dollars in 2009. Out of this total, the proceeds of transnational organized crime would be considered being 1.5 % of the global GDP, 70% of which would likely have been laundered through the financial system[87].

In our times, a "successful" state does not only require the harmonious superposition of a Nation over a territory. It must also be economically sustainable; hence the temptation of some territories and states to trade their sovereignty in order to attract the necessary capital ensuring their development. Tax evasion, money laundering, and grand corruption benefit from the financial opacity then organized which in turn distorts the global economy[88].

What to conclude from the last two years events? According to the audit from FINMA, the Swiss Financial Market Supervisory Authority, conducted as part of the identification of the assets held by the three Arab leaders ousted, 4 of the 20 Swiss banks examined were not following, sometimes crudely, prudential rules in their relationships with 'politically exposed persons' (head of State, ambassadors, heads of public enterprises, members of their entourage, etc).

A similar audit conducted by the FSA, the UK Financial Services Authority stated, *"Serious weaknesses identified in banks' systems and controls, as well as indications that some banks are willing to enter into very high-risk business relationships without adequate controls when there are potentially large profits to be made, means that it is likely that some banks are handling the proceeds of corruption or other financial crime"*[89].

Ultimately, the Wachovia, Sal-LCB banks, Standard Chartered, Crédit Suisse, or HSBC cases are only the consequences of a bigger picture, Licit and illicit finances, far from excluding one another, responding to the law of supply and demand, tend to attract each other.

This is where the opacity organized by some states and territories creates a bridge between legal and illicit economies. This bridge, this service, is used for tax evasion, grand corruption, and money laundering alike.

Of course, this leads to further increasing the tax burden on fair tax payers contributing for the others. In emerging countries, this fuels the gap between rich and poor. This also has an impact on the euro zone crisis.

In its 2011 report, Transparency International saw in the economic difficulties of the euro zone the *"inability of the government to fight against corruption and tax evasion. In Germany and France, official estimates of losses due tax fraud are around 30 billion euro a year, which represent a third of their respective annual deficit. In comparison, in countries where tax evasion is seen as*

---

[86] *Los Angeles Times*, "Global Population Growing Faster than Expected, U.N. says", July 10, 2013.

[87] UNODC, *Estimating Illicit Financial Flows resulting from Drug Trafficking and other Transnational Organized Crime*, Press Release, October 25, 2011.

[88] Mickaël R. Roudaut, *Géopolitique de la crise, des monnaies et de la fraude*, Op. cit.

[89] FSA, *Banks' Management of High Money-laundering Risk Situations*, June 2011, 94 p. spéc. p. 6.

Illicit Markets: A Big Business (in U.S. dollars)

To view images, scan codes with phone,
or visit http://pso.site50.net/Roudaut_Figure_6.png

Source: Global Financial Integrity, *Transnational Crime in the Developing World*, February 2011, 56.

The counterfeiting estimate excludes counterfeits produced and sold locally (i.e., within the same country) as well as illegal downloading.

"The Biggest Money Laundering Fines in Millions of Dollars"

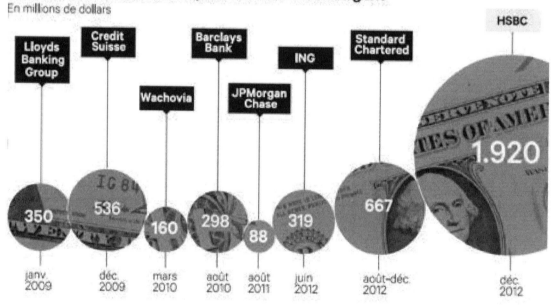

Source: *Les Echos*, 12 Dec. 2012

endemic and the most hit by the euro financial crisis, the amount of revenue loss is of the same magnitude as the amount of the annual deficit"[90].

If fraud and tax evasion are of course not the "only explanation" to the crisis in the euro zone, they are a cause of its lasting effect. That is why one of the keys to the fight against money laundering, tax evasion, and grand corruption lies in the transparency of legal entities so as to prevent them from being a vehicle to fraud[91].

Positive evolution, the current financial crisis, helped in creating momentum, notably within the G20 and in Europe, on the impacts of financial opacity.

Beyond, money laundering is found to have played a role in the Mexican (1994–1995) and Thai (1997) financial crises, further highlighting the global stability concern raised by the illicit economy[92].

Conclusion

While the international community concerns tend to remain focused around terrorism and weapons of mass destruction, the illicit economy became both a suppletive and an alternative model of development attracting a new type of criminals, state. Yet, by lack of awareness, the links between crime, illicit trades, economy, and states remain poorly studied and rarely debated[93].

Even though a global and national security concern, transnational organized crime and illicit trades remain too often confined to a law enforcement issue. Clearly, there is a need to fundamentally rethink the way organized crime is defined and understood.

As for the recent political will displayed against financial opacity, it has yet to pass the test of time.

---

[90] *Le Monde*, December 1, 2011.
[91] Michael Findley, Daniel Nielson, and Jason Sharman, *Global Shell Games: Testing Money Launderers' and Terrorist Financiers' Access to Shell Companies* (World Bank, 2012), 33, *The puppet Masters*, October 2011, 284.
[92] Guilhem Favre, "Prospering on Crime: Money Laundering and Financial Crisis", *Centre for East and South-East Asian Studies*, 2005.
[93] A welcome initiative, the OECD launched in 2012 new activities aiming to quantify the impacts of illicit trade and the illegal economy on economic growth, sustainable development and global security.

The Impact of Victimological Theories on the Rights of Crime Victims in France
Robert Cario

Victimological theories emerged as an inevitable element of the criminological observations (Pinatel 1975; Debuyst et al. 1998 and 2008) which surrounded their creation at the beginning of the 1950s. Due to the state of scientific knowledge at the time, these theories had a very narrow focus on the characteristics of the act, the mechanisms of committing a crime, and the personality of the perpetrator[1] alone. Nevertheless, they began contributing to the strengthening of victim rights, which until then had exclusively focused on repairing bodily and material damage. Undeniably, over recent decades, victimological theories have helped to promote the ongoing humanization of criminal proceedings. This benefits all concerned by the crime suffered/committed, from the protagonists themselves to society as a whole, including the numerous parties who contribute to a cross-disciplinary strategy of prevention, control, and optimum harmonious treatment of the criminal phenomenon (Cario 2008).

This study essentially aims to evaluate the rights of (potential or real) victims of crime, throughout the criminal process, by examining contemporary criminal and penal policies in light of victimology. The reparation of the damages suffered has always followed more or less vindictive procedures (of elimination) or vindicatory ones (of reciprocity, sharing, and reconciliation). It cannot be said that responses to crime have historically been based on the first of these, with the second belonging more to a supposedly civilized world. Although it is not possible to precisely define how far a civilization is concerned about human dignity, particularly the dignity of those who may be involved in crime, it seems that these two methods of resolution/regulation of conflicts between subjects have always existed, or even coexisted. They continue today, although symbolically, in view of the assertion of the fundamental principles of criminal law, the proclamation of human rights, and the implementation of crime-fighting policies which are far less concerned with retribution than with taking people into account (Laingui and Lebigre 1979 and 1980; Carbasse 2006; Garnot 2009; Zehr 1990).

Despite its imperfections (particularly the social status of the person concerned), the adversarial system long allowed for consideration of the victim, whose active involvement was a necessary element in any criminal procedure. Although the inquisitorial system had its advantages (the state initiated proceedings, in principle for the benefit of all victims), it excluded the victim from procedures which directly concerned them. However, in both cases, many criminal conflicts were "resolved" without any official litigation by tradition or law. The pervasiveness of infrajustice throughout our criminal history cannot be denied.

---

[1] The term *perpetrator* should be used only to refer to people who have broken the criminal norm (whatever it may be), for at least two key reasons: the first lies in the temporal and geographical variability of criminal systems, and the second in the presumption of innocence that protects those who have not been proven guilty. Obviously, it may refer to people carrying out a sentence of imprisonment or a sentence within society.

However, it is more accurate to speak of alternations and superimpositions: the complexity of the criminal phenomenon irremediably condemns any reductionist approach to human behaviors, criminal or otherwise. It seems that the criminal justice system is permanently being reconstructed, in conceptual, praxeological, and practical terms, driven by the ever-renewed desire to provide the fairest possible trial (Garnot 2009).

In order to achieve such a democratic ambition, which is undoubtedly legitimate, necessary, and promising, complementarity between criminology (of the aggressor and the victim) and criminal law (substantial, formal, and regarding sentence enforcement) is required. Aside from the incontestable statement that the criminal situation precedes the very creation of the repressive "norm," there can be no competition between these disciplinary fields. However, many interdisciplinary schools of thought refuse to acknowledge these obvious facts, irrespective of the scientific approach to crime via a cross-disciplinary rationale.

The impact of victimological theories on the rights of victims has become particularly apparent over recent decades. Nevertheless, this impact remains difficult to describe, because (oddly), the victim is not legally defined,[2] with the science dedicated to him her not receiving any more unanimous definition from legal doctrine.[3] Nevertheless, it is improved scientific understanding of victims that has allowed their ethical rights, and more recently their procedural rights, to be recognized. Firstly, classical theories fitted into the positivist epistemic framework, which took issue with the notion of the judge placing criminal responsibility on the accused once he or she has been held accountable for the action in question. The degree to which the victim may be to "blame" in the perpetration of the act was therefore of prime importance in the eyes of the first victimologists, as part of efforts to calculate the extent of the perpetrator's guilt. Scales of guilt led to classifications, which were soon criticized for their sometimes caricatured nature. However, other proposals are worth comparing to the most rational of the theories that succeeded them (primarily Von Hentig 1948; Ellenberger 1954; Mendelsohn 1956; Fattah 1967).

Secondly, reacting sometimes excessively to research on the criminal-victim pairing, feminist victimologists aggressively

---

[2] See, however, article 2 (which must be enshrined in French law by November 16, 2015) of Directive 2012/29/EU (October 25, 2012) by the European Parliament and Council, setting out the minimum standards for victim rights and for crime-victim support and protection. This directive replaces Council Framework Decision 2001/220/JHA, according to which "For the purposes of this Framework Decision: (a) 'victim' shall mean a natural person who has suffered harm, including physical or mental injury, emotional suffering or economic loss, directly caused by acts or omissions that are in violation of the criminal law of a Member State." This can be compared to Cario (2012, 39), according to whom "Any person who suffers must be considered a victim. a) These sufferings must be personal, real, and socially recognized as unacceptable; b) and must justify support for the persons concerned, ranging (depending on the circumstances) from the nomination of the act or event, to participation in the procedures for revealing the truth, legal information, medical care, psychotherapy, psychological or social support, and compensation."

[3] See Cario (2012) pages 42 and particularly 44: "Victimology, a branch of criminology, can be defined as the multidisciplinary scientific discipline concerned with the overall analysis of victimizations, in their individual, collective, and social dimensions, in their emergence, their process, their consequences, and their repercussions, in order to favor their prevention and, where necessary, bodily, psychological, social, and/or material reparation for the victim and/or their family."

contested this "art of blaming the victims." This in itself gave rise to an initial and very productive epistemological break, without which victimology would undoubtedly not have survived. Wishing to understand the harm done to women as a whole, they set up victimization inquiries (following the very popular model of the self-confession investigations reserved for possible criminals). The results were unique and highly relevant. They allowed the first "profile" of victims to be drawn up, permitted systematic examination of the reasons for which victimization is not reported, and allowed for a clear description of the stigmatizing experience inflicted on victims by the legal apparatus in its wider sense.

Based on these successive achievements over a matter of just decades, victimologists from the 1980s onwards developed scientific approaches to the hidden side of crime, using constantly updated knowledge from the neurosciences, psychology (in the wider sense), sociology, and recently, restorative victimology. The latter, with its global approach to the criminal phenomenon, seems able to reconcile the various penological and criminological doctrines, which some still see as strictly opposed and incompatible. In fact, available research confirms the true proximity between the protagonists, at least as concerns the infractions of our basic social values (crimes and serious offenses involving violence, deception, or force).[4] They are shown to be close in terms of instability and vulnerability (which may be personal, emotional, familial, educational, professional, social, cultural, or spiritual), as well as in relationship terms (in the vast majority of crimes against people, the protagonists know one another). These shared types of vulnerability, in environments that may be unavoidable (the family), coincidental (school and peer group), or chosen (living environment), often make the roles of victim and perpetrator interchangeable, creating an almost fatal cycle which our exclusionary societies are unable to break (or do not wish to, where the causes are known).[5] Such social brutality, which is intolerable in a democracy, must give rise to essentially preventative criminal and penal policies, and where these fail, to policies of resocialization. Anyone wishing to engage in scientific study of this subject, without giving in to background penal populism, knows very well that penalties depriving perpetrators of their freedom, although necessary for serious offenses (which account for 20% of criminal convictions—and therefore 0.5% of offences—in France), are extremely counterproductive in fighting recidivism. This is true as concerns the time in prison itself (Kensey and Tournier 2005; Kensey 2007; Tournier 2010; Kensey and Benaouda 2011) and also as concerns the cross-disciplinary or multiprofessional individualization of the sentence, which is essential for progressive and effective reintegration

---

[4] It is useful here to remember that French criminal law does not explicitly define criminal offenses other than via a classification by seriousness (as crimes, offenses, and infringements (article 111-1 of the French Penal Code). In its criminological sense, "crime takes the form of a breach of a value established as fundamental for the human, cultural, and social wellbeing of members of a group in which the conflict emerges," (Cario 2008, 191).

[5] The first victimologists were not unaware of most of these different factors. They included the random allocation of the roles of criminal and victim, fair and full compensation for victims, multidisciplinary clinical assessments, and the importance of protagonists' vulnerabilities. Nevertheless, given what is known today, science cannot validate the emphasis that "victimology of the act" places on the fault of the victim (particularly in cases of sexual violence against women) or "predispositions" (specific or general) to become victims.

into society.[6] A survey conducted in 2009, but published in June 2013(!),[7] examining a representative sample of the French population, revealed that three-quarters of people asked did not believe that prison was an effective way of combating recidivism. As a logical consequence, 64% were in favor of adjustments to sentences.

France's 1808 Criminal Procedure Code officially allowed crime victims to bring civil proceedings before the criminal courts. This is particularly envied in common law, where the victim has only witness status. Nevertheless, it was not until the second half of the twentieth century, when the necessary accompanying rights were introduced, that it really became possible for victims and their families to seize this important opportunity, and obtain full and effective compensation. This evolution has only really become visible and measurable over the last four decades. The 1980s was the decade of the right to recompense for damages suffered (fixed in 1977, then full and nonsubsidiary from 1990). The 1990s saw the introduction of the right to victim support, with victim support services created from 1982, and federated within the National Institute for Victim Support and Mediation (Institut national d'aide aux victimes et de médiation: inavem.org) from 1986. The first decade of the 2000s were ones of the *rationalization of victim rights*, particularly with regard to their subjective rights. The circular of July 13, 1998, brought the first reasoned criminal policy on victims. The first public policy for victim support was drafted out in the Lienemann report, submitted to the prime minister on March 29, 1999. The law of June 15, 2000, was largely inspired by this report, and aimed to set out a real status for crime victims. The 2010s seemingly are attempting to move towards the restorative approach to crime. In this approach, both the victim and the perpetrator (as well as their family and the communities to which they belong) are placed at the heart of the available measures (including community, legal, psychological, and/or social measures), in a taming (Saint-Exupéry 1943) or adaptive approach. The most promising illustrations of this, complementing the dominant penal response (which is currently too inflationary), have been restorative meetings like mediation, family group conferences, sentencing circles,[8] and detainee-victim meetings, despite the avoidable risk of them being exploited (on this evolution, see Cario 2001; Lopez, Portelli, and Clément 2007; Strickler 2009; Ministère de la Justice et des Libertés 2012; D'Hauteville 2013).

Without such a strategy of inclusion, involvement, and collaboration of all those wishing to take part, being put in place by trained professionals, the whole penal chain, social reintegration attempts, overall reparation, the restoration of social peace (regarding the protagonists, those around them, and society as a whole), and the reestablishment of social harmony can be nothing more than wishful thinking (Zehr 2002; Cario 2010). Although it is not possible to describe all the dimensions of the impact of victimological theories on victim rights, it nevertheless seems appropriate to examine their interconnections chronologically and on two levels, namely looking at repairing

---

[6] Incarceration also significantly worsens the inequalities already suffered by prisoners in terms of health and family life, both during and after imprisonment. On this, see Wildeman and Muller (2012).

[7] Belmokhtar and Benzakri (2013). See also Lévy (2013), which refers to a 2011 issue of Infostat Justice entitled "Les Français et la prison" (2009 survey), not listed as such in the collection.

[8] On this, see § 46 of Directive 2012/29/EU, to be enshrined in French law before November 16, 2015.

the damage caused by the crime, and the role given to victims and/or their families throughout the penal process.

A – From Compensation Alone to the Right to an Overall Remedy for Crime Victims

Compensation of the victim or their loved ones has always been a priority in dealing with the damages caused by the transgression of a value that the social group considers should be protected. Within various methods and procedures, compensation has taken the form of noxal surrender, voluntary arrangements, equivalents, or financial transactions. These "damages and interests" have more recently become a recognized right before the criminal or civil courts. France's 1958 Criminal Procedure Code (which substantially altered the 1808 Code) thus allows the victim to receive civil redress for their damages before the criminal judge, if desired. Thanks to this institutionalization of civil action, the victim can be compensated for all damages suffered and, just as importantly, participate in bringing out the truth and fighting impunity.[9] The second of these "two faces of civil action before criminal courts"[10] is still problematic for some aspects of legal doctrine, inadequately influencing case law, and retaining only its "vengeful" aspect in the strictly vindictive sentence. Current victimology allows for the rejection of such an approach to victimhood: in the daily life of the courts, the victim is in a far more vindicatory position, in which they ask to understand what has happened (often within the small family circle), and thus avoid this type of crime or serious offense being repeated, and participate in the search for solutions together with the perpetrator (where appropriate), in order to be reconciled. The most inadmissible vindictive attitudes are undeniably present in everyday court life, but they are very rare. They are mostly the result of the parties having been insufficiently supported in the aftermath of the events, or of bad management of the case, resulting in secondary victimization at various stages of the penal process. The fate of victims of petty offenses or contraventions (which are very unfairly sanctioned) gives even greater cause for concern: most of the time, they are forgotten in alternatives to judicial proceedings, and unseen by the qualified tribunals, because the acts are perceived not to be serious. Consequently, the victims' rights are sacrificed on the altar of merciless criminal inflation. Consequently, the huge benefits of massive, urgent decriminalization that conforms to the fundamental principles of criminal law (particularly necessity, proportionality, and rapidity) seem easy to imagine.

Since 1970, the Council of Europe has included compensation for crime victims as an issue on its work program. French law provides remarkable legislation in this domain, offering one of the most effective compensation systems in the world (1977, 1986, 1990, 2008; art. 706-3 and s., R 50-1 and s. C.pr.pén [Criminal Procedure Code]). Together, the Compensation Board for the Victims of Crimes (Commission d'indemnisation des victimes d'infractions, or CIVI: civil jurisdiction, independent) and the Guarantee Fund for Victims of Terrorism and other Offences (Fonds de

---

[9] According to article 2 of France's Code of Criminal Procedure, "Civil action to claim reparation for damages caused by a crime, offense, or infringement is a right of all those who have personally suffered from the harm directly caused by the infraction."

[10] See Boulan (1973).

garantie des victimes d'actes de terrorisme et autres infractions, or FGTI, funded by a €3.30 deduction on all property insurance contracts; see www.fgti.org), ensure that victims and/or their loved ones are rapidly compensated by the national community after the event.[11]

A tripartite regime currently applies in France.[12] For the most serious offenses (art. 706-3 *C.pr.pén.*), full and unconditional compensation is available for recognized damages. This is the case for death, permanent disability, or total personal disability lasting one month or more, human trafficking, rape, sexual assault, or sexual interference with a minor under fifteen years of age. Several less serious offenses may also result in compensation (art. 706-14 *C.pr.pén.*), in certain circumstances (capped or subsidiary compensation, possibilities of payment by third-party payers, means testing, or serious psychological and material situations). This may apply for theft, fraud, breach of trust, extortion, and destruction or damage to property. More questionably (as there is a risk of FGTI impoverishment, and it would be preferable to systematize the "personal accidents guarantee," as a "social provision" benefiting the most vulnerable), victims filing civil suits, not admissible before the CIVI, can call upon the Recovery Assistance Service for Victims of Offenses (Service d'aide au recouvrement des victimes d'infraction, or SARVI, art. 706-15-1 *C.pr.pén.*), in order to obtain payment of damages and interests accorded by the criminal judge (where the condemned is insolvent or refuses to pay).

In practical terms, any person[13] who has suffered harm as a result of voluntary or involuntary acts of a criminal nature can file a claim for compensation, with the necessary supporting documents, to the CIVI registrar. This must be completed within three years of the offense or within a year of the legal decision. The registrar immediately passes the claim to the FGTI, who must make a compensation offer to the victim within two months. Following agreement and approval, within two months of the settlement proposal from the CIVI president, the sums awarded are paid within one month. Otherwise, the judicial procedure continues as normal before the CIVI, or even the trial judge. Like provisions during the proceedings, the aforementioned jurisdictions can award additional sums if further disadvantage is caused (Tisserand 2012).[14]

There is great debate concerning the issue of the victim's responsibility. However,

---

[11] Accidents at work, road traffic accidents, and hunting accidents are covered by other, equally effective compensation systems.

[12] Victims or their families can also choose the traditional civil tribunal or the criminal tribunal, for example by direct summons of the accused. These courses of action (subject to specific time limits) are not without major disadvantages for the victim, who must offer proof of the accused's acts and of their sufferings in the first case, and wait for the final decision in the second (in which they are only a witness, unless they launch civil action, thus placing them back in the above scenario, which is by far the most effective one).

[13] All victims (and their families) of French nationality or who are citizens of an EU Member State are eligible when the offense is committed in France. Similarly, a foreign victim can be eligible if they are residing legally at the time of the events or of their request. Only a victim with French nationality can obtain compensation for offenses committed abroad.

[14] This case law particularly applies to ongoing domestic violence, where the spouse under attack reacts by killing the violent partner and where it is not possible to plead legitimate defense. See in particular the Supreme Court of Canada's decision in the emblematic "R. v. Lavallée" affair (1990) 1 SCR 852/21022, scc.lexum.org. See also (in France) the Cour d'Assises du Nord's acquittal ruling of March 23, 2012 (Guillemin affair), in Pascale Robert-Diard, prdchroniques.blog.lemonde.fr.

it is necessary to differentiate between two, nonreducible situations. In civil proceedings before the CIVI, blame on the part of the victim can reduce or exclude their (and/or their family's) right to compensation. This may be the case, for example, where the victim provokes the accused using insults or threats (sometimes under the influence of various toxic products), and in cases of score settling in large-scale crime. In criminal law, the issue is somewhat trickier. The first victimologists suggested that victim responsibility should be taken into account, constructing highly controversial typologies. Penal decisions may still discharge or acquit of the perpetrator, when the crime is committed in response to domestic abuse (Fattah 2004; Fattah 2011).

The everyday observations of practitioners within victim support services in particular, relayed by victimological doctrine, have further broadened the field of redressable damage, both in nature and in terms of the sums paid. A wide range of temporary, permanent, current, and future damages are taken into account. The right to reparation is first of all available for economic damages as a result of losses suffered in the wider sense: medical costs, loss of independence, and practitioner's fees (for doctors, lawyers, and so forth). Similarly, compensation is available for lost profits (mainly job loss, incapacity to work, loss of opportunities, and a child's loss of amenity). Compensation can also be obtained for nonpatrimonial damages. Since these relate to the person, they are not subject to payment from a third-party payer. Temporary functional deficit concerns reduced quality of life (suffering, fear, withdrawal, and so forth). Permanent functional deficit primarily includes disfigurement and the inability to indulge in certain activities (leisure, sexual pleasures, procreation, starting a family, anxiety linked to waiting, and so forth).

The theoretical and clinical impact of victimology is also seen in the right to compensation for damages for specific offense situations and/or their consequences in the short or long term. For example, compensation for victims of terrorism and their families has changed greatly, particularly thanks to the work of the founder of the victim association SOS-Attentats (Rudetzki 2002; Rudetzki 2004), who is now "terrorism delegate" within France's National Federation for Victims of Collective Attacks and Accidents (Fédération nationale des victimes d'attentats et d'accidents collectifs, fenvac.org). The epidemiological inquiries carried out at the request of SOS-Attentats in 1987 and 1989 specifically emphasize that severe physical, psychological, and social suffering (primarily post-traumatic stress, ongoing effects on hearing, loss of social and professional aptitude, and lasting depression) can continue for varying and extended periods of time after the event. This is particularly worrying in terms of public health. These very complicated, collective victimizations require immediate and high-quality medical and psychological intervention, via the establishment of multidisciplinary teams who are specifically trained to help these physical and/or psychological victims. Exclusively, the suffering of victims of terrorist attacks still justifies reparation for specific harm, set at 40% of the capital for partial permanent incapacity, with a minimum of €2,300. It is also worth examining several additional particularities concerning the compensation rights of entitled persons, particularly for harm caused by the media (for example use of photographs taken on the site of an attack), and for the psychological distress, problems in the living community, and frequent medical visits related to dealing with the suffering of a dying loved one (Cario 2013). The "security and terrorism" law of December 21, 2012, responded to other demands from victims and their representatives. These included the application of French criminal law to acts committed abroad by a French person or a person normally residing within the French territory, the entitlement to the common right to damage claims in criminal proceedings within one year of the criminal court's decision on the public or civil action to be taken,[15] and the inclusion of the phrase "died to serve the nation" or "victim of terrorism" on the death certificate (giving the person's children the status of wards of the nation).

A further example of the impact of victimological works and practices comes from applying knowledge acquired on the postcrime state of stress to victims of serious offenses, thus broadening their right to compensation. It is now proven that victims of serious offenses suffer varying degrees of trauma (a true psychological injury) as a result of the psychological damage that the criminal act inflicts. Trauma is entirely unpredictable, and depends on the individual's perceptions, resistance, aptitudes, and social-support resources. The suffering provoked by the event can lead to a state of stress, which is generally short lived and may or may not be specific, or even to a state of confusion over the days following the criminal act. However, the trauma can cause deep psychological injuries when the subject faces the prospect of death (physically or psychologically in cases of rape), their own imminent death, or that of a loved one or any other person. Thus, the terror of this precise moment (shock, inability to think, a blank mind) is a key symptom of a trauma that might characterize traumatic neurosis (Lebigot 2005; Kédia and Sabouraud-Séguin 2008). These various problems are listed in clinical tables under "acute stress disorder" (ASD), and "post-traumatic stress disorder" (PTSD).[16] While the symptoms of ASD disappear fairly rapidly, those of trauma are buried within the psychic apparatus, and may only resurface much later, following a latent period, depending on the individual and the situation. The trauma may therefore cause symptoms such as repetition, personality change, traumatic dreams, fatigue, sadness, daytime memories, character alteration, low self-esteem, dissociative episodes (flashbacks), permanent alertness, family/relationship/professional conflicts, various inhibitions, phobic avoidance, drug addiction, depression, and various psychosomatic illnesses (Herman 1992; Brillon 2004; Guay and Marchand 2006; Josse 2011; Guay and Lopez 2013). Fortunately, psychological care for those concerned has developed on these bases within the criminal justice system itself, via highly original and effective care initiatives. These include the creation of multidisciplinary medico-psychological emergency units which intervene on the sites of attacks or offenses (Cario 2010), and highly innovative and effective therapeutic practices (Damiani and Lebigot 2011).

One final example demonstrates this rich collaboration between victimologists and criminologists. Although it is so far perhaps the least advanced, it has nevertheless brought remarkable changes in professional legal practice (in the wider sense), regarding the consideration of the social repercussions of victimization. Under the joint impetus of police and victim support professionals, the mid-1970s saw the introduction of social workers in police stations,

---

[15] Submissions to the FGTI formerly had to be made within ten years of the attack. The new law allows the FGTI Administrative Council to reopen cases for legitimate reasons.

[16] See "DSM-V" (dsm5.org) or "CIM 10" tables (who.int).

[17] See article L 121-1-1 of France's social action and families code (code de l'action sociale et des familles, introduced by the law of March 5, 2007), which legitimizes their status.

first in Chartres, then in Limoges. Now in place at 180 locations, mainly in urban and periurban environments, this "new" profession,[17] which is still poorly funded, provides a very satisfactory response to the needs and responsibilities of all involved. These social workers are specifically trained in social intervention. They are responsible for meeting and listening to those who come to police stations or teams, and for responding to their needs using a network of partners: medico-judicial bodies, accommodation and social rehabilitation centers, victim support services, and health and/or social organizations. They are in constant demand, due to a pressing social need and penal victimizations (particularly within families), and they offer a tailored and coordinated response, as soon after the event as possible. Given the criminological complexity of social distress or crime situations that these social workers face, it is highly desirable for them to belong to a victim support service (aniscg.org). It is in this spirit of multidisciplinary action immediately following the event that the emergency victim support service was created in the 2000s.

This strategy of providing social support as soon as the events come to light is indispensable. The victimization suffered further aggravates the victim's situation, and that of those close to them. It may result in marital and even family issues (exacerbated by not being able to rapidly express the feelings provoked by the victimization); problems at work (either technical or in working relationships) which may lead to absenteeism; job loss, or resignation (when the victimization took place in the victim's mode of transport or at work); inevitable socioeconomic problems (when the victim's professional and social abilities are affected); relationship problems (particularly related to the difficulty of publicly assuming the harmful consequences of the crime and/or the victimization); dropping out of school; and antisocial behavior on the part of children and adolescents. This accumulation of consequences is worse when the offense is a serious one, involving the loss of a loved one (Rossi 2013), a physical or psychological attack with serious consequences, rape, or even an attack on property which ruins the victim and/or their family. They may also lead to social dependency, isolation, rejection, and even social exclusion. Scientific research is required into these potential social repercussions, which are still largely neglected today. Their consideration offers immediate benefits for victims and/or their families, as well as long-term advantages for society (reduced expenditure), thus showing that social work plays an essential role in the short-, mid-, and long-term support for issues involving family, work, and the social reintegration of victims and their families.

More generally, the most recent studies emphasize that in order to represent emotions, it is necessary to remember them as realistically as possible. It seems that the "social sharing of emotions" facilitates this, since others' words add new meanings to those that the victim attributes to the traumatic event (Rimé 2005). Such a representation is even more indispensable for victimizations within the family environment, in order to help the victim escape the tyrannical hold of their aggressor, to whom they are emotionally linked and on whom they are often socioeconomically and culturally dependent. Thus, beyond the victim's own individual recovery through social sharing of their emotions, the emotional relationships between humans reinforce and contribute to strengthening social harmony in general. This is why it is necessary to constantly resituate the trauma in a wider victimological context, in order to fully take the victim into account.

Based on observations in victimology and victim support, specific provision should be made for real, professional victim-assistance initiatives (legal, judiciary, psychological, and social ones), in the immediate, short-term, mid-term, and even long-term aftermath of the event. In contrast to the victimizing passivity of the protagonists which still characterizes criminal procedures, it is therefore important to allow victims and their families to become as active as they are willing and able to in dealing with the consequences and repercussions of the infringement, which present severe dangers for social harmony.

B – From Representation Alone to the Empowerment of Crime Victims

The move towards overall reparation for victims of offenses and their families seems to be the best example of effective collaboration between victimologists, jurists, victim support professionals, the police, magistrates, and (more generally) all of those socio-judiciary players involved in the prevention, control, and treatment of the criminal phenomenon, including as legislators. However, effectiveness (the criminal justice system's capacity to assume the staffing and resource costs of these three complementary missions) is not necessarily synonymous with efficiency (be it pragmatic, in order to resocialize and make amends to those concerned, symbolic for the purposes of restoring social peace, or educational in order to ensure respect for the protected value and legitimate punishment for transgressions). The proof lies in the permanency of the attenuated but still insidious forms of secondary victimization, which are highly destabilizing and even traumatizing. The only effective defense against these aberrations is the professionalism of the various people who recognize the human dignity of the victim and/or their loved ones and allow them to exercise their rights fully and easily.

In this sense, it is notable that works in victimology were quick to observe the perverse manifestations of secondary victimization. Feminist victimologists showed, during victimization investigations (which they were the first to develop), that victims suffered entirely unjust secondary victimization at the hands of by the criminal justice system, from police to judge (be it an investigating judge, a trial judge, or an enforcement judge) (Symonds 1980; Baril 2002; Gaudreault 2004). Moreover, this serious neglect of victims, which slows their referral to the relevant authorities to address their suffering, is common and threatens both their dignity and the principles of a fair trial. Victims suffer derision (in response to the reported facts), provocation (regarding the "credibility" of their claims), scorn (concerning the consequences of the affair and the trial process), and abandonment (regarding the recovery of compensation awarded).

Just as importantly, the works of feminist victimologists have allowed victims to finally be recognized through their sufferings, whether the offence is reported or not, and even if it is dismissed during the proceedings. After classical assertions on "victimogenic" factors, these investigations allowed them to systematize the personal and social characteristics of crime. In this sense, and schematically, the most serious victimizations mostly take place not in public transport or parking lots, but in the family home itself. Consequently, in most cases, the victim knows their aggressor. In short, victims live in various and severe situations of vulnerability. Marital and sexual violence is, as a rule, chronic and extremely victimizing (Baril 2002). The links between violence committed and suffered are highly apparent. More specifically, the main reasons for victimizations not being reported to the relevant authorities are clearly identifiable: the victims are vulnerable, they fear reprisals, they are ashamed to reveal what they have suffered or been unable to prevent, and they fear or do not understand the solutions available to them.

In light of these works, it is unsurprising that their authors rightly assert the need to develop far more sophisticated ways of dealing with offenses, undoubtedly on the juridical-penal level (sanctioning the perpetrator and compensating the victim), but also and even more so on the psychological and social levels (supporting the victim, and healing trauma). Thus, during the 1960s, the first victim support services emerged in the Anglo-Saxon countries, for victims of (mostly male) violence, such as domestic mistreatment and sexual violence. In France, the first such services were created in the early 1980s. Today, their work is broader, extending to all types of offenses and gender of the perpetrator.

In the same vein, victim representation by law professionals at all stages of the criminal procedure, the low importance given to their words, and their very place in the courtroom have all made victims passive, invisible, and powerless. Such inhumanity in "taking charge of" victims (with various players using their powers to speak for them) has given way (although still not entirely) to their being "taken into account" (with various players using their powers to help them exercise their rights), via a "one-stop shop" strategy. Today, all professionals know that if the victim's sufferings are not recorded when they are first revealed, it will be very traumatizing for them to return to them, because "repeating is redoing and reliving." This is why it is so important to have truly competent frontline professionals, and readily available technical recording methods.

From an ethical point of view, all victims have a set of three rights which are inherent to their victimized-person state, and which are not dependent on any criminal procedure. These rights have two aims: to guarantee their human dignity and the rights connected to it, and to reinforce their role as active subjects. Concerning the latter aspect, it is necessary to overcome the widespread confusion between the victim's "role," "status," "place," and "state." It goes without saying that victims should never be able to lose their state as a person. Nevertheless, crime deeply and sometimes lastingly shakes life's most fundamental beliefs: that the world around us is benevolent, that it is well ordered (has meaning), and that we are part of it as a harmonious contributor. In order to give (back) meaning to their lives, victims need to understand what has happened to them, and what they might have done to prevent it. If victims lack answers, they will tend to blame themselves and other people. Unable to regain control over their own lives, they lose their self-esteem, and feel degraded and dehumanized, thus becoming even more vulnerable (Janoff-Bulman 1992; Luminet 2008; Williams and Poijula 2013; Horowitz 2013). In order for a victim wanting to regain control to be able to take on this kind of role, they must be given a specific status, made up of subjective rights that regulate their situation, independently of any proceedings or criminal courts. Similarly, if the victim so wishes, they must be offered a place throughout the criminal proceedings and take a clear position in the courtroom space. However, this must be on the condition that they are given the possibility of escaping the traditional passive role to which the criminal justice system still confines them, so that they can finally regain active control over their life as a subject (having been robbed of this by the crime).

The victim's right to **recognition** ensures that their state as a suffering person is taken into account. This is a fundamental ethical position. Recognition from others is the basis of the victim-subject's and the perpetrator-subject's humanity: "The me is awakened by the grace of the you" (Bachelard 1935). According to Axel Honneth (1992), social-recognition relationships are structured around three characteristics pertaining to love (a vector of self-confidence), rights, (a vector of self-respect), and social solidarity (a vector of self-esteem). Recognition is therefore "based on the experience of intersubjectivity [which supposes that] the relationship is more important than the individual" (Guéguen and Malochet 2012).

The **support** of those involved is an essential accompaniment to recognition. Supporting someone means linking oneself to them to go where they go, at the same time as them, and at their pace. It also means empathetic sharing of the sufferings of the protagonists—certainly those of the victim, but also those of the perpetrator. Placed at the center of the process of consideration, the victim is the only person who knows the suffering he or she has experienced; he or she is the only person who knows the direction that needs to be taken, and what the crucial problems that need to be faced are and what his or her needs are to be able to resolve those problems (Rogers 1961).

Reparation must be total, full, and effective. It means taking care of oneself and of the other as a victimized person, taking into account the complexity of all that has been suffered. Material compensation is necessary, but it is not enough (see above). Psychological and social reparation, where necessary, must also come into play. Similarly, in criminal proceedings, full participation as an active subject offers both procedural reparation and, once the decision is final, symbolic reparation through naming and separation (of acts and persons).

Should it be emphasized that these ethical positions must also benefit the perpetrator, who, however serious his or her acts, is still a person with fundamental human rights, to whom the major procedural principles must also apply? Should it be emphasized that these rights and principles must be shared by the immediate and close communities to which the protagonists belong, as well as more widely by all citizens? If this is not the case, any attempts to restore the social bond will remain wishful thinking.

Thanks to the work of victim support practitioners (in the broadest sense) and researchers in victimology, new needs have been identified. These have finally allowed legislators to allocate a "status" to victims of offenses. Thus, in order not to remain little known or unknown, the victim must have free and quick **access to the law**. All democratic societies must introduce initiatives to provide this. Similarly, obtaining legal aid consolidates the recognition of every victim's right to the valuable defense of a lawyer. The victim can choose between civil proceedings (an ordinary judge or the crime-victim compensation commission) or criminal proceedings (direct proceedings, an ordinary complaint, or a complaint with a claim for criminal indemnification). Taking civil action offers real guarantees to victims of crimes or serious offenses (the proportionality principle must apply), or their entitled persons. It does this by allowing them either to engage public action (by means of action), or to become a part of it (by means of intervention). Although this is an important right, victims can still struggle to fully exercise it in everyday practices.

It is just as important to respect the rights of victims to **be received**, **speak**, and

be listened to. The conditions in which the victim is received are essential to their recognition, from the moment they report the offense, to the execution of court decisions. There is a need for dedicated, adapted premises, with the necessary technical equipment (for audiovisual or digital recordings of hearings), in order to record the first, always difficult, moments in which the victim recalls their experience. These must help to avoid repetition of the painful circumstances of the victimization further down the line. In all of these locations, multidisciplinary teams or specially trained personnel must be available to listen to victims and help them express themselves, during the physical and psychological ordeal of recounting their experiences. Such an ability to listen and, above all, to reformulate what the victim has expressed does not come naturally: it requires specialist training and continuing professional development. If they cannot share the painful emotions created by the crime, victims become highly frustrated and struggle to understand. They may experience doubts about the usefulness of the process and the real gravity of the events, or feel that the criminal justice system is defending its own interests. The victim's statements need to be heard and believed, as part of the presumption of victimhood. There is nothing more traumatizing than having one's words doubted, without nuance or precaution. They also need to be understood (if necessary, via an interpreter). This needs to happen at a pace that spares them physical and psychological fatigue, and irreproachable professional methods need to be observed.

All victims have the right to **help** in the form of emergency financial or material assistance, when such resources exist. Dedicated funds should be made available to victim support services in particular, so that they can meet the immediate material needs after the offense: cash, hotel bookings, and taxis home, for example. Moreover, citizen support from trained volunteers in the hours immediately following the victimization should be promoted, to meet needs such as collecting children from school, checking whether any domestic constraints might cause additional distress, securing premises after burglary in agreement with the local authorities, and driving the victim to the various locations where their victimization will be addressed.

All victims have the right to **be informed** about the results and characteristics of the proceedings that might be engaged, be they criminal, civil, administrative, or disciplinary. They must therefore be able to call upon any relevant institutions or services. Information also has an influence on the victim's precise rights in getting their demands met, as regards the situation of the perpetrator and their punishment. This requires widespread victim support services, "one-stop shop" registries, forensic units, and legal advice centers which are adapted to the specific characteristics of territories. Also important in this respect is the recent extension of the judge delegated for victims, assisted by a victims' bureau, to all regional courts. Primarily, the role of victim support services seems to be primordial in assisting victims in the wider sense, in terms of legal information, and psychological and social help. The huge decrease in public funding is incomprehensible, given the needs so frequently expressed by victims, and the savings that could be made by offering immediate professional support following the event.

All victims have the right to **protection** from the perpetrator, and all necessary measures must be taken to avoid contact. To achieve this, the perpetrator can be banned from receiving, meeting, or entering into contact with the victim in any way, with the victim then being told about this ban. Today, great controversy surrounds the question of the victim's place during the execution of sentences. Victims are still not allowed to take part in this process, and it is the responsibility of sentencing-enforcement bodies to ensure their protection. The victim must also be protected from the media, because the public hunger for "social reality" can lead media professionals to go beyond the deontological framework of the objective right to inform, without the full consent of those concerned. More professional protection is required during legitimate extension measures for condemned parties, which force those involved to relive the suffering of their victimization in an unacceptable manner, long after the events and the trial. At the same time, the very presence of the media in places where the freed person is accommodated makes true reintegration almost impossible.

Along these lines, as soon as victims and their loved ones decide to take legal action, they are guaranteed specific rights, and remarkably, when they are placed in a position to exercise them, as emphasized above, the criminal trial becomes a source of procedural and symbolic reparation. These rights, guaranteed in an equitable and balanced way to the parties, offer them the possibility of fully assuming their active role as a legal subject, rather than remaining confined to that of an object in the proceedings (as is all too often the case today). Overlaps between fundamental, ethical, victim, and procedural rights are inevitable.

The right to **a fair criminal trial** is one of the key achievements of the last century, during which international recognition of human rights has nevertheless failed to prevent the massacres of civilian populations that still occur around the world (Cario 2013). Nevertheless, as the fundamental principles of criminal law, human rights are a crucial part of our criminal justice systems. Thus, a fair trial requires a balance to be achieved between the rights of the perpetrator and those of the victims. It is based upon the importance and necessity of respecting all of the rights mentioned above. The equality of resources between all of the protagonists must also be respected at all stages of the proceedings (art. 6, European Convention on Human Rights) (Moderne 2012; Renucci 2012). Victims who file civil suits can also ask for various measures to be taken under France's Criminal Procedure Code. These include free access to the case files, requests for hearings, meetings, site visits, expert assessments and second opinions, and recourse against decisions made at all stages of the procedure (except for criminal appeals where civil interests are not involved).

The **rights of defense** must therefore be rigorously guaranteed to the victim, and strictly upheld. A quality defense allows the victim to truly participate in the procedure. The broadening, revaluation, and (even better) the systematization of legal aid for victims cannot be avoided, because national solidarity is expected to help them and to assume the ever-growing costs of criminal proceedings. When necessary, victims who are minors must also be represented by an ad hoc administrator. Local agreements between the bar and the victim support service greatly facilitate the defense (in terms of legal advice) and support (in terms of legal information, the trial process, and assistance at hearings) of victims. In current legislation, such agreements, which ensure complementarity between roles, are designed to better share the advantages of restorative justice measures, such as mediation benefiting adults as well as minors.

All of those encountered during the criminal procedure must be **truly competent professionals**, who offer high-quality services. Although most are competent in their own area of expertise, they still need to be given greater awareness of the criminal issue (in initial and continuous training), on site and behind the scenes of the crime. The complexity of human behaviors, particularly aggressive behaviors, means that in order to understand, take into account, and meet the needs of those involved, it is necessary to have the most up-to-date knowledge in criminology and victimology. Complementarity between the various professionals is a real asset, as long as each of them offers their expertise without confusion between roles. The integrated coming together of responses to the victim's needs consolidates their recognition and improves reparation. No professional confidentiality should be allowed to cover the failure to assist a person who is in danger, especially where such assistance will benefit the victimized person. This makes it absolutely necessary to include criminology in the university training of teachers, researchers, and professionals concerned by ethics and deontology, providing up-to-date theoretical and practical knowledge, in a spirit of cross-disciplinarity and as part of an enlightened partnership. Yet this obvious fact is still disputed in France, as a result of out-of-date ideologies or clique mentalities.

On the other hand, all victims also have **duties**. They must therefore respect the impositions of the law and act within the appropriate period, if they wish to take legal action. All victims also have the duty to respect the institutions or services with which they come into contact, cooperating faithfully, and carrying out certain steps themselves. More generally, victims should make a point of bringing direct or indirect offenses against them to the attention of the relevant authorities. Similarly, great caution should be observed when lodging complaints, because if they are found to be unjustified, the person making the complaint may be held civilly liable. If the complaint is abusive, there may be sanctions for defamation following closure of the case, a refusal of information, a nonsuit decision, discharge, or acquittal. More generally, the victim and their entitled persons or family must respect the perpetrator and their family as persons possessing fundamental human rights.

In conclusion, victimology theories have a significant and almost unquestionable impact on the rights of victims, at least in France. Their integration, mostly via current criminal law, is extremely important. Whatever those in charge may think, complementarity between the scientific approach to crime and the social reaction that it requires is not only viable, but also effective. Much has been achieved in this domain, but many obstacles still remain.

The restorative approach to conflicts and their regulation highlights many of these obstacles, allowing us to prevent or react to them (Wright 1996; Zehr 1990; Zehr 2002; Johnstone 2003; Gailly 2011). Beginning from acts committed/suffered, it also (and perhaps above all) encourages us to deal with the experiences of each of the protagonists, beyond the act itself. Such an all-encompassing strategy cannot be blind to the need to empower those involved, wherever desired. Specially trained professionals who take into account the legal, psychological, and social consequences of crime therefore offer the most promising route back to lasting social harmony. We must not give in to the pessimism of thought: the optimism of action as a strategy for reacting and acting must provide the route, here and now, to achieving this humanist objective.

Robert Cario serves as emeritus professor of criminology and is the former director of the Jean Pinatel Unit for Comparative Criminology at the Université de Pau et des Pays de l'Adour. He has been elected president of the new French Institute for Restorative Justice (www.ifjr.org)

References and Further Reading

Bachelard, Gaston. 1935/1992. "Préface." In *Je et tu*, edited by M. Buber, 8–9. Paris: Aubier Montaigne.

Baril, Micheline. 2002. *L'envers du crime*. Paris: L'Harmattan.

Belmokhtar, Zakia. and Abdellatif. Benzakri. 2013. "Les Français et la prison." *Infostat Justice* 2013-6-122.

Boulan, Fernand. 1973. "Le double visage de l'action civile exercée devant les juridictions répressives," *JCP* I, 2563.

Bouzat, Pierre, and Jean Pinatel. 1970. *Traité de droit pénal et de criminologie*. Paris: Dalloz. (See especially volume 3 (1975).)

Brillon, Pascale. 2003. *Comment aider les victimes souffrant de stress post-traumatique?* Québec, Les éditions Quebecor.

Carbasse, Jean-Marie. 2006. *Histoire du droit pénal et de la justice criminelle*. Paris: PUF.

> Cario, Robert. 2001. "Victimes d'infraction." In *Répertoire de droit pénal et de procédure pénale*, edited by Maurice Aydalot, Pierre Arpaillange, and Frank Jacques Laederich. Paris: Dalloz.
> - 2008. *Introduction aux sciences criminelles. Pour une approche globale et intégrée du phénomène criminal*. Paris: L'Harmattan.
> - 2010. *Justice restaurative. Principes et promesses*. Paris: L'Harmattan.
> - 2012. *Victimologie. De l'effraction du lien intersubjectif à la restauration sociale*. Paris: L'Harmattan.
> - 2013. "L'Indemnisation des victimes d'actes de terrorisme en droit français." *AJpénal* 2013-5: 264–269.
> - and S. Ruiz. 2014 (in press). *Droit(s) des victims*. Paris: L'Harmattan.

Damiani, Carole and François Lebigot, eds. 2011. *Les Mots du trauma. Vocabulaire de psychotraumatologie*. Ph. Duval.

D'Hauteville, Anne 2013. In *Une Certaine idée de la criminologie*, edited by Pierre V. Tournier, 135–150. Paris: L'Harmattan.

Debuyst, Christian, Françoise Digneffe, and Alvaro Pires. 1998. *Histoire des savoirs sur le crime et la peine*, Vol. 2, *La rationalité scientifique et la naissance de la criminologie*. Brussels: De Boeck Université / Ottawa: Presses de l'Université; Montréal: Presses de l'Université.

Debuyst, Christian, Françoise Digneffe, and Alvaro Pires. 2008. *Histoire des savoirs sur le crime et la peine*, Vol. 3, *Expliquer et comprendre la délinquance* (1920–1960). Brussels: De Boeck / Larcier.

DIV. 2008. *Les intervenants sociaux en commissariat de police et groupement de gendarmerie. Guide pratique*. Paris: Les Ed. de la Direction interministérielle à la ville (DIV).

Ellenberger, Henri. 1954. "Relations psychologiques entre le criminel et la victime." In *R.I.C.P.T*: 103–121.

Fattah, Ezzat Abdel. 1967. "Vers une typologie des victimes." *Revue Internationale de Politique Criminelle*: 164.

———. 2004. "Positions savantes et idéologiques sur le rôle de la victime et sa contribution à la genèse du crime." In *La victime est-elle coupable? Autour de l'Œuvre d'Ezzat Abdel Fattah*, edited by Robert Cario and Paul Mbanzoulou, 23-41. Paris: L'Harmattan.

———. 2010. "Quand recherche et savoir scientifique cèdent le pas à l'activisme et au parti pris." *Criminologie* 43 (2): 49-88.

Gailly, Philippe. 2011. *La justice restauratrice*. Brussels: Larcier.

Garnot, Benoît. 2009. *Histoire de la justice. France, XVIè-XXè siècle*. Paris: Gallimard.

Gaudreault, Arlène. 2004. "Victimisation secondaire." In *Dictionnaire de sciences criminelles*, edited by Gérard Lopez and Stamatios Tzitzis, 960-963. Paris: Dalloz Ed.

Guay, Stéphane, and André Marchand, eds. 2006. *Les troubles liés aux événements traumatiques. Dépistage, évaluation et traitements*. Montréal: Presses de l'Université de Montréal.

Guay Stéphane, and Gérard Lopez. 2013. "Traitement du stress posttraumatique et de ses troubles connexes." In *Traité des violences criminelles Les questions posées par la violence et les réponses de la science*, eds. Maurice Cusson, Franca A. Cortoni, and Stéphane Guay, 887-909. Montreal: Hurtubise.

Herman, Judith. 1992. *Trauma and Recovery. The Aftermath of Violence—From Domestic Abuse to Political Terror*. New York: Basic Books.

Horowitz, Mardi Jon. 2013. *Stress Response Syndromes. PTSD, Grief, Adjustment, and Dissociative Disorder*. North Vale, NJ: Jason Aronson Inc.

Janoff-Bulman, Ronnie. 1992. *Shattered Assumptions: Towards a New Psychology of Trauma*. New York: Free Press.

Johnstone, Gerry, ed. 2003. *A restorative justice reader: texts, sources, context*. Cullompton: Willan.

Josse, Evelyne. 2011. *Le traumatisme psychique. Chez le nourrisson, l'enfant et l'adolescent*. Brussels: De Boeck.

Kédia, Marianne and Aurore Sabouraud-Seguin. 2008. *Psycho-traumatologie*. Paris: Dunod.

Kensey, Annie. 2007. *Prison et récidive. Des Peines de plus en plus longues: la société est-elle vraiment mieux protégée?* Paris: Armand Colin.

——— and Abdelmalik Benaouada. 2011. "Les risques de récidive des sortants de prison. Une nouvelle évaluation." *Cahiers d'études pénitentiaires et criminologiques* 36. www.justice.gouv.fr.

——— and Pierre Tournier. 2005. *Prisonniers du passé? Cohorte des personnes condamnées, libérées en 1996-1997: examen de leur casier judiciaire 5 ans après la levée d'écrou*. Paris: Adm. Pénitentiaire.

Ministère de la Justice et des Libertés. 2012. *Les droits des victimes*. Paris: Min. Justice. www.justice.gouv.fr

Lévy, Jean-Daniel. 2013 "Le Rôle des médias et de l'opinion publique sur la question de la récidive." Paper presented at the Conférence de consensus sur la prévention de la récidive, Paris, February 14–15. conference-consensus.justice.gouv.fr.

Lopez, Gérard, Serge Portelli, and Sophie Clément. 2007. *Les droits des victimes. Droits, auditions, expertise Clinique*. Paris: Dalloz.

Luminet, Olivier. 2008. *Psychologie des émotions. Confrontation et évitement*. Brussels: De Boeck Ed.

Mendelsohn, Benjamin. 1956. "Une nouvelle branche de la science bio-psycho-sociale." *R.I.C.P.T.* 2: 95–109.

Moderne, Franck. 2012. *La Convention européenne des droits de l'homme*. Paris: Dalloz.

Pignoux, Nathalie. 2008. *La Réparation des victimes d'infractions pénales*. Paris: L'Harmattan.

Renucci, Jean-François. 2012. *Traité de droit européen des droits de l'homme*. Paris: LGDJ-Lextenso.

Rimé, Bernard. 2005. *Le partage social des émotions*. Paris: P.U.F. Quadrige.

Rossi, Catherine. 2013. *Homicide: les proches des victimes*. Paris: L'Harmattan.

Rudetzki, Françoise. 2002 "Œuvre de justice: histoire d'un combat." In *Victimes: du traumatisme à la restauration*, edited by Robert Cario, 219–255. Paris: L'Harmattan.

Rudetzki, Françoise. 2004. *Triple peine*. Paris: Calmann-Lévy.

Saint Exupéry, Antoine de. 1943. *Le Petit prince*. Paris: Gallimard/Folio.

Strickler, Yves, (ed.) 2009. *La place de la victime dans le procès pénal*. Brussels: Bruylant.

Symonds, Martin. 1980. "The Second Injury to Victims." *Evaluation and changes*, special issue: 36–38.

Tisserand, Thierry. 2012. "Le Mécanisme d'indemnisation des victimes." In *Psycho-criminologie*, eds. Jean-Louis Senon, Gérard Lopez, and Robert Cario, 417–425. Paris: Dunod.

Tournier, Pierre V. 2010. *Dictionnaire de démographie pénale. Des outils pour arpenter le champ pénal*. Paris: L'Harmattan.

Von Hentig, Hans. 1948. *The Criminal and His Victim. Studies in the Sociobiology of Crime*. New Haven, CT: Yale University Press.

Wildeman Christopher and Christopher Muller. 2012. "Mass Imprisonment and Inequality in Health and Family Life." *Annual Review of Law and Social Sciences* 8: 11–30.

Williams, Mary Beth, and Soili Poijula. 2013. *The PTSD Workbook: Simple, Effective Techniques for Overcoming Traumatic Stress Symptoms*, Oakland, CA: New Harbinger.

Wright, Martin. 1996. *Justice for Victims and Offenders. A Restorative Response to Crime*. Winchester: Waterside Press.

Zehr, Howard. 1990. *Changing Lenses: A New Focus for Crime and Justice*. Scottdale, PA: Herald Press.

2002. *The Little Book of Restorative Justice*. Intercourse, PA: The Good Books.

States of Change: Power and Counterpower Expressions in Latin America's Criminal Insurgencies
John P. Sullivan

Sustained penetration by transnational criminal networks (cartels and gangs) of state institutions is challenging Mexico and states throughout Latin America. This paper discusses 'criminal insurgencies' as a power-counterpower dynamic where criminal combatants use violence, corruption, and information operations (including new media) to challenge state capacity and legitimacy, and exert territorial control for supporting their illicit economic domains. Social/environmental modification, including information operations (e.g., narcocorridos, narcomantas, and narcopintas), alternative belief systems (i.e., narcocults), targeted symbolic violence (including attacks on journalists and government officials), direct attacks on the police and military by criminal bands (sometimes wearing uniforms), and the provision of social goods while adopting the mantle of social bandit or primitive rebel are stimulating a new narcocultura. This paper examines these irregular conflicts through a comparative ethnographic lens to inform intelligence analysis and practice supporting an understanding of strategic shifts in sovereignty and governance.

Transnational criminal networks (cartels and gangs) are challenging Mexico and Latin America. Technology, especially Internet Communications Technology (ICT) and "new media," provides potentially powerful tools for actors on all sides of the conflict. New media can be used to transmit *narcocultura* to support penetration of state institutions. New media also influences the struggle for state authority and can both empower and constrain transnational criminals. Violence, corruption, and information operations (including new media) are culminating as a force with the potential to challenge state capacity and legitimacy (solvency). Together they are an important element of the emergence of new state-forms and tool of criminal insurgencies in contested zones. To assess this situation, I will briefly look at attacks on journalists (or narco-censorship), *narcocultura*, and social banditry, and information operations (info ops) as a means of stimulating a new *narcocultura*. I will view these through the lens of criminal insurgency (Sullivan 2012) and co-opted state reconfiguration (CStR) (Garay Salamanca and Salcedo-Albarán, 2010; 2011).

Transnational Illicit Networks and State Transition

According to Moisés Naím (2006), transnational criminal organizations (TCOs) operate on a global scale and derive economic and political power from their broad reach and accumulation of wealth. Gayraud (2005) observes that these organizations have abandoned operating from the margins and now seek to operate at the core of political and economic systems becoming a central driver of conflict. Indeed, the United Nations Office on Drugs and Crime reports on the "Threat of Narco-Trafficking in the Americas" (UN-

ODC October 2008) and "The Globalization Of Crime: A Transnational Organized Crime Threat Assessment" (UNODC June 2010) highlight the impact of transnational crime on states. According to the 2008 report, both states and communities are caught in the crossfire of drug-related crime and the violence that it fuels in the Americas and across the Atlantic to Europe and Africa.

The resulting conflicts have been characterized as a battle for information and real power (Manwaring 2008; 2009). These state challengers—irregular warriors/non-state combatants (i.e., criminal netwarriors)—increasingly employ barbarization and high order violence, combined with information operations, to seize the initiative and embrace the mantle of social bandit (Hobsbawn 2000) in order to confer legitimacy on themselves and their enterprises. Sovereignty is potentially shifting or morphing as a result of these challenges.

Mexico and Latin America as Laboratory for New Media in Contested Zones

Mexico and Latin America are currently experiencing a serious onslaught from organized crime (cartels and gangs) that challenges and erodes state capacity to govern, negates the rule of law through endemic impunity, and drives humanitarian crises through high-intensity violence and barbarization. In Mexico, ~50,000 persons have been killed in the crime wars between 2006–2011 according to analysis by the Trans-Border Institute (Molzhan, Rios, and Shirk 2012). New media is central to this quest for power. In this essay, I will briefly summarize the interactive impact of violence, corruption, and information operations to sustain concerted assaults on state solvency (which I view as the net result of capacity and legitimacy). I view these assaults as criminal insurgency, a contemporary form of conflict where crime and politics merge. As such, cartel information operations are an expression of power-counterpower dynamics (Castells 2009).

The role of new media in drug war and criminal insurgency includes:

- the ability to communicate in real and/or chosen time, by all parties in the conflict;
- a means of providing warnings and signaling intent;
- a means of overcoming narco-censorship;
- a means of enabling traditional media reportage, as well as an alternative to traditional media;
- a mechanism to enable civil society and/or *narcocultura*.

Violence, Corruption, and Info Ops

It is no surprise that organized crime groups (gangs and cartels) use violence as a tool in the course of business. Threats, coercion, and instrumental violence punctuate their activities. That said, these enterprises usually seek to elude detection and prefer co-opting (corrupting) the instruments of state rather than engaging in direct confrontation. Organized crime usually operates in a state of what Sabet (2009) calls 'collusive corruption'. Yet, as the current crime wars illustrate, these actors can directly confront the state when their interests are challenged (Bailey and Talyor 2009). Criminal insurgency is the mechanism of the confrontation with the state that results when relationships between organized crime and the state fall into disequilibrium.

One key element of the security threat resulting from disequilibrium is the impact of transnational gangs and cartels on sovereignty where illicit networks try to reconfigure states. Such reconfiguration could include erosion of state capacity (or the exploitation of a state solvency gap), corrupting and co-opting state organs (government, the police, and the judiciary) in all or part of the state—through the development of criminal enclaves—or at the extreme edge, state failure. State reconfiguration is potentially a more common outcome than abject state capture or state failure and co-opted state reconfiguration (CStR) where the cartels and gangs use a range of actions to obtain social, economic, political, and cultural benefits outside the effective control of the state (Garay Salamanca and Salcedo-Albarán 2010; 2011). Criminal insurgency is the means of effecting CStR; this process is currently in play in Brazil's favelas, Mexico, and many parts of central America (El Salvador, Guatemala, and Honduras).

Criminal Insurgency

Criminal insurgency presents a challenge to national security analysts used to creating simulations and analytical models for terrorism and conventional military operations. Criminal insurgency is different from conventional terrorism and insurgency because the criminal insurgents' sole political motive is to gain autonomy and economic control over territory. They do so by hollowing out the state and creating criminal enclaves to maneuver.

The capture, control, or disruption of strategic nodes in the global system and the intersections between them by criminal actors can have cascading effects. The result is a state of flux resulting in a structural "hollowing" of many state functions while bolstering the state's executive branch and its emphasis on internal security. This hollowing out of state function is accompanied by an extra-national stratification of state function with a variety of structures or fora for allocating territory, authority, and rights (TAR). These fora—including border zones and global cities—are increasingly contested, with states and criminal enterprises seeking their own 'market' share. As a result, global insurgents, terrorists, and networked criminal enterprises can create 'lawless zones,' 'feral cities,' and 'parallel states' characterized by 'dual sovereignty.' Criminal insurgencies can exist at several levels (Sullivan 2012):

- *Local Insurgencies* (gangs dominate local turf and political, economic, and social life in criminal enclaves or other governed zones).
- *Battle for the Parallel State* (battles for control of the 'parallel state.' These occur within the parallel state's governance space, but also spill over to affect the public at large and the police and military forces that seek to contain the violence and curb the erosion of governmental legitimacy and solvency).
- *Combating the State* (criminal enterprise directly engages the state itself to secure or sustain its independent range of action; cartels are active belligerents against the state).
- *The State Implodes* (high intensity criminal violence spirals out of control; the cumulative effect of sustained, unchecked criminal violence, and criminal subversion of state legitimacy through endemic corruption and co-option. Here, the state simply loses the capacity to respond).

Attacks on Journalists

As noted in "Attacks on Journalists and "New Media" in Mexico's Drug War: A Power and Counter Power Assessment" (Sullivan 2011):

> An increasingly significant component of this violence has been directed against journalists and media outlets in an effort to silence the media so the cartels can operate with impunity. Television stations (such as Televisa in Tamaulipas and Nuevo León) have been attacked with grenades, journalists assassinated, kidnapped or disappeared. According to the Committee to Protect Journalists (2010), at least 30 journalists have been killed or disappeared in Mexico in the past four years, and 11 have been killed this year [2010] alone. A detailed map tracking violence against Mexican journalists has been developed by The Knight Center for Journalism in the Americas at the University of Texas, Austin (Knight Center 2010).

As I have previously recounted, on September 18, 2010, Ciudad Juárez's newspaper *El Diario* (currently edited across the international frontier in El Paso) printed an unprecedented editorial ¿Qué quieren de nosotros? In English, simply "What do you want from us?" Published the day after one of its photographers was murdered, the editorial provides a stark illustration of the intense assault against Mexico's free press by cartel gangsterism. The *El Diario* editorial (translation at *Los Angeles Times*, La Plaza) read in part:

> Gentlemen of the different organizations that are fighting for the Ciudad Juarez plaza, the loss of two reporters of this news organization represents an irreparable breakdown for all of us who work here, and in particular, for our families.
>
> We'd like you to know that we're communicators, not psychics. As such, as information workers, we ask that you explain what it is you want from us, what you'd intend for us to publish or to not publish, so that we know what is expected of us.
>
> You are at this time the de facto authorities in this city because the legal authorities have not been able to stop our colleagues from falling, despite the fact that we've repeatedly demanded it from them. Because of this, before this undeniable reality, we direct ourselves to you with these questions, because the last thing we want is that another one of our colleagues falls victim to your bullets.

Here we see the raw response to cartel info ops and narco-censorship. This pattern is repeating itself in a brutal fashion. As noted in the companion paper to this piece:

> An increasingly significant component of this violence has been directed against journalists and media outlets in an effort to silence the media so the cartels can operate with impunity. Television stations (such as Televisa in Tamaulipas and Nuevo León) have been attacked with grenades, and journalists assassinated, kidnapped or disappeared. One of the most visceral artifacts of the cartel counter-power struggle is brutal attacks on journalists. According to Article 19, in 2011 there were 172 attacks on journalists in Mexico. These figures include 9 murders of journalists, 2 murders of media workers, 2 disappearances of journalists, and 8 assaults with firearms or explosives against media facilities or installations (Article 19 2012). Since 2000, 66 journalists have been killed, 13 journalists have disappeared, and 33 media buildings or facilities have been targets of explosive or firearm attacks (Article 19 2012).

As I recounted in my 2011 paper on cartel info ops (Sullivan 2011):

> News blackouts have become a feature of the Mexican drug war. This has two facets: government information operations and cartel info ops. According to the Knight Center, "coverage of drug trafficking in Mex-

ico has been based generally on an official view of the facts...Releasing information a bit at a time allows Mexico's government to construct a public image of winning the war" (Medel 2010, 22). Coupled with cartel efforts to obscure their hand through instrumental attacks and threats against journalists, the resulting pressure has resulted in near complete media blackouts in some areas.

The Fundación MEPI (Fundación Mexican de Periodismo de Investigación) recently completed a six-month study of 11 regional newspapers in Mexico to gauge the impact of cartel interference or influence on reportage of cartel crime. The Fd. MEPI study relied on content analysis of the papers' coverage and interviews with journalists. The report found that the regional newspapers were failing to report many cartel/narco crimes. In order to conduct the study, Fd. MEPI constructed a list of execution-style murders tied to cartel actions and then compared it to regional coverage. In all regions, the number of stories mentioning cartel violence from January to June 2010 amounted to a small fraction of the actual incidents. Consider for example that cartel murders in Ciudad Juárez averaged an estimated 300 per month in 2010, but during the study period El Norte, the regional paper mentioned less than 10% or 30 per month. The impact appears even greater in eastern Mexico, where El Mañana in Nuevo Laredo published only 3 stories out of a potential 98 in June. Areas controlled by the Gulf and Zeta (e.g., Taumalipas) cartels appear particularly impacted by the cartel blackout effect with between 0-5% of cartel violence stories reported.

The Fd. MEPI analysis is presented in Table One. Specifically, it reviewed the crime stories published in January-June 2010 from the following newspapers: El Noroeste (Culiacán), El Norte (Ciudad Juárez), El Dictamen (Veracruz), Mural (Guadalajara), Pulso (San Luis Potosi), El Mañana (Nuevo Laredo), El Diario de Morelos (Morelos), El Imparcial (Hermosillo), La Voz de Michoacán (Morelia), and Milenio (Hidalgo). In 8 of the 13 cities studied, the papers reported only one of every ten narco violence stories; in the cities with more reportage, only 3 out of 10 were published.

The cartels do not seek simple silence and impunity, they notably seek to influence perception, using a type of "narco-propaganda." This strategy employs a range of tools. These include both violent means—beheadings, *levantóns* (kidnappings), assassinations, bombings, and grenade attacks—and informational means—*narcomantas* (banners), *narcobloqueos* (blockades), *manifestacións* (orchestrated demonstrations), and *narcocorridos* (or folk songs extolling cartel virtues). Simple physical methods such as graffiti and roadside signs are now amplified with digital media.

Narcocultura and Social Banditry

The concept of social/environmental modification is based on research into cartels and "*narcocultura*" by Robert J. Bunker and others (Bunker 1997; Bunker and Bunker 2010a; 2010b; Hazim 2009a; 2009b) and reportage on the "Santa Muerte"[1] and "Jesús Malverde" cults by Guillermoprieto (2009) and La Familia Michoacana cartels with its own theological practice by Logan and Sullivan (2009). Guillermoprieto (2009) defines *narcocultura* in a broad sense as a "twisted relationship with power" often exemplified by corruption. In a social or cultural context—the one we are examining

---

[1] While Santa Muerte is often translated into English as Saint Death, a more accurate translation would be "Sacred Death" or "Holy Death."

here—she defines *narcocultura* in a narrower sense: *the production of symbols, rituals, and artifacts—slang, religious cults, music, consumer goods—that allow people involved in the drug trade to recognize themselves as part of a community, to establish a hierarchy in which the acts they are required to perform acquire positive value and to absorb the terror inherent in their line of work.*

According to Bunker and Bunker (2010b), social environmental modification is an element of non-state warfare; specifically: "This warfare—manifesting itself in 'criminal insurgencies' derived from groups of gang, cartel, and mercenary networks—promotes new forms of state organization drawn from criminally based social and political norms and behaviors." Key elements of social/environmental modification include alternative worship or veneration of "narco-saints," symbolic violence (including beheadings and corpse messaging—i.e., attaching a message to a corpse), the use of *narcocorridos* (epic folk songs), and social media to spread messages and confer legitimacy of a cartel. Womer and Bunker (2010) mention the importance of social media in social environmental modification in the context of gangs and Mexican cartels. A notable example of a band crafting *narcocorridos* extolling the virtues of cartels is *Los Tigres del Norte*.[3] Other forms of messaging conferring potential legitimacy or shaping public perception include *narcomensajes* (essentially communiqués), *narcomantas* (placards and banners), and *manifestacions* (demonstrations).

Together these means can be combined to cast legitimacy on the cartel or gang in a form of post-modern 'social banditry' as described by Hobsbawn (2000).

Narcocultura and social banditry are mechanisms for securing cartel and gang legitimacy in the areas they seek to dominate. They join raw violence and barbarization as tools of social domination and a means of accumulating and solidifying political power (Sullivan and Elkus 2011). Cartel info ops thus not only seek to silence adversaries and criticism, they become means of extending political reach and reconfiguring the state to a structure that furthers its objectives. Here cartels both use and are confronted by new media. As they seek to gain legitimacy—or submission—from the populace on the one hand (also providing utilitarian social goods in furtherance of this objective), civil society seeks to strike back and retain order and security on the other. Here we see cartels broadcasting their brutal attacks, wearing cartel uniforms,[4] and developing and deploying their own encrypted microwave communications networks[5] to spread their words and deeds.

Conclusion: The New Narcocultura and Intelligence

Cartels and gangs are essentially non-state violent actors. When they conduct operations they clearly display a range of signatures that can be detected by assessing their transactions to discern their intent and tactical, operational, and strate-

---

[3] According to Guillermoprieto, Los Tigres del Norte originated in Sinaloa and emigrated to California where they play norteño music with corrido lyrics glorifying narcotraffickers.

[4] See Kelly Vlahos, "Bloody Mexican Gangs Make It 'Official,' with Uniforms, Insignia," *Fox News*, May 23, 2011.

[5] See Ronan Graham, "Mexico Seizes 'Zetas' Communications System," *InSight* Crime, December 2, 2011 and "Marines dismantle Los Zeta communications network in Veracruz," *Borderland Beat*, September 8, 2011.

gic objectives. Identity intelligence is one approach to assign their tactical and operational disposition and the position of cartel/gang actors within the illicit networks. This can be reinforced through red team analysis (Sullivan and Elkus 2009).

Narcocultura enables the cartels by transmitting their strategic (and tactical/operational) status; identity intelligence (I2) and social network analysis can help translate this into an understanding of the group's current status, order of battle, operational tempo (optempo), and intended targets (for operational purposes and campaigns to control territory). Not only can new media enable the cartels/gangs and their civil society rivals, it can empower intelligence and enforcement operations. As new media (horizontal mass communications)—as seen in micro-blogs (Twitter), YouTube, Facebook, and blogs such as *NarcoRed, El Blog del Narco*, and *CiudaDanaMtySur* (an excellent site for monitoring real-time attacks)—helps mitigate the impact of narco-censorship, it can also fuel real-time situational awareness and intelligence analysis. Understanding and exploiting new media is an essential tool for addressing criminal insurgency, co-opted state reconfiguration, and shifts in sovereignty.

References:

Article19. 2012. "Increases in 2011 Attacks on Journalists, The Authorities Still Do Not Do Their Job." PRESS RELEASE, Mexico City, 20 March.

Bailey, John., and Matthew M. Taylor. 2009. "Evade, Corrupt, or Confront? Organized Crime and the State in Brazil and Mexico." *Journal of Politics in Latin America 1* (2):3–29.

Bunker, Pamela L., Lisa J. Campbell, and Robert J. Bunker. 2010. "Torture, Beheadings, and Narcocultos." *Small Wars & Insurgencies* 21 (1):145–178.

Bunker, Robert. 2011. "The Growing Mexican Cartel and Vigilante war in Cyberspace." *Small Wars Journal*, November 3. On line, no volume.

Castells, Manuel. 2009. *Communication Power*. Oxford: Oxford University Press.

El Diario. 2010. ¿Qué quieren de nosotros?, Editorial, September 18 . http://www.diario.com.mx/notas.php?f=2010/09/18&id=6b-124801376ce134c7d6ce2c7fb8fe2f (Translated at *Los Angeles Times, La Plaza*, September 24, 2010).

Fundación MEPI. 2010. "México: La nueva espiral del silencio." 17 November.http://fundacionmepi.org/narco-violencia.html.

Gayraud, Jean-François. 2005. El G9 de las Mafias en el mundo. Geopolítica del crimen organizado. Barcelona: Ediciones Urano.

Guillermoprieto, Alma. 2009. "The Narcovirus." *Berkeley Review of Latin American Studies* (Spring), 2–9.

Hazim, Hakim. 2009a. "Mexico's Seeds of Radicalization: Micro Movements with Macro Implications." *GroupIntel*, 17 August. http://www.groupintel.com/2009/08/17/mexico's-seeds-of-radicalism-micro-movements-with-macro-implications/.

Hazim, Hakim. 2009b "Santisma Muerte: A Troubling Trend in Radicalization." *GroupIntel*, 23 February.http://www.groupintel.com/2009/02/23/santisma-muerte-a-troubling-trend-in-radicalization/.

Hobsbawn, Eric. 2000. *Bandits*. New York: The New Press.

Knight Center for Journalism in the Americas. 2010. Google Maps/*Knight Center Map of Threats Against Journalists in Mexico*. Austin: University of Texas. http://maps.google.com/maps/ms?ie=UTF8&hl=en&msa=0&z=6&msid=103960216204540664660.00048f4d-72b6a3a226539 and http://knightcenter.utexas.edu/blog/new-knight-center-map-pinpoints-threats-against-journalism-mexico.

Logan, Samuel, and John P. Sullivan. 2009. "Mexico's Divine Justice." ISN Security Watch, ETH Zurich, August 17, 2009.

Manwaring, Max G. 2008. *A Contemporary Challenge to State Sovereignty: Gangs and Other Illicit Transnational Criminal Organizations (TCOs) in Central America, El Salvador, Mexico, Jamaica, and Brazil*. Carlisle Barracks: Strategic Studies Institute, January.

Manwaring, Max G. 2009 *A "New" Dynamic in the Western Hemisphere Security Environment: The Mexican Zetas and Other Private Armies*. Carlisle Barracks: Strategic Studies Institute, September.

Medel, Mónica. 2010. *Journalism in Times of Threats, Censorship and Violence*, Report from the Seminar "Cross-border Coverage of U.S.-Mexico Drug Trafficking," March 26–27, Knight Center for Journalism in the Americas at the University of Texas at Austin, Sponsored by the McCormick Foundation.

Naím, Moisés. 2006. *Illicit: How Smugglers, Traffickers and Copycats are Hijacking the Global Economy*. New York: Anchor Books.

Sabet, Daniel. 2009. "Confrontation, Collusion and Tolerance: The Relationship Between Law Enforcement and Organized Crime in Tijuana." *Mexican Law Review* 11 (2):3–29.

Salamanca, Garay, Luis Jorge and Eduardo Salcedo-Albarán. 2010. *Illicit Networks Reconfiguring States: Social Network Analysis of Colombian and Mexican Cases*. Bogotá: Metodo.

Salamanca, Garay, Luis Jorge, and Eduardo Salcedo-Albarán, Eds.. 2011. "*Drug Trafficking, Corruption and States: How Illicit Networks Reconfigure Institutions in Colombia, Guatemala and Mexico*." Pre-published draft.

Sullivan, John P. 2008. "Criminal Netwarriors in Mexico's Drug Wars." *GroupIntel*. December 22, 2008. http://www.groupintel.com/2008/12/22/criminal-netwarriors-in-mexico's-drug-wars/.

Sullivan, John P. 2010a. "Criminal Insurgencies in the Americas." *Small Wars Journal*, February 13, 2010.

Sullivan, John P. 2010b. "Cartel Info Ops: Power and Counter Power in Mexico's drug War." *MountainRunner*. 15 November. http://mountainrunner.us/2010/11/cartel_info_ops_power_and_counterpower_in_Mexico_drug_war.html.

Sullivan, John P. 2011. "Attacks on Journalists and "New Media" in Mexico's Drug War: A Power and Counter Power Assessment." *Small Wars Journal*, April 9.

Sullivan, John P. 2012. "From Drug Wars to Criminal Insurgency: Mexican Cartels, Criminal Enclaves and Criminal Insurgency in Mexico and Central America, and their

Implications for Global Security." *VORTEX Working Papers*, No. 6, Bogotá, Colombia: Scientific Vortex Foundation, March.

Sullivan, John P., and Adam Elkus. 2009 "Red Teaming Criminal Insurgency." *Red Team Journal*, 30 January. http://redteamjournal.com/2009/01/red-teaming-criminal-insurgency-1/.

Sullivan, John P., and Adam Elkus. 2010. "Cartel v. Cartel: Mexico's Criminal Insurgency." *Small Wars Journal*, February 1.

Sullivan, John P., and Adam Elkus. 2011. "Barbarization and *Narcocultura*: Reading the Evolution of Mexico's Criminal Insurgency." *Small Wars Journal*, August 31.

Sullivan, John P., and Carlos Rosales. 2011. "Ciudad Juárez and Mexico's 'narco-culture' Threat." *Mexidata*. 28 February. http://mexidata.info/id2952.html.

Sullivan, John P., and Adam Elkus. 2012. "Mexican Drug Lords vs. Cybervigilantes and the Social Media." *Mexidata*. March 5, http://mexidata.info/id3288.html.

Trans-Border Institute (Molzhan, Cory, Virdiana Rios and David Shirk). 2012. Drug Violence in Mexico: Data and Analysis Through 2010. San Diego: University of San Diego, March.

United Nations Office on Drugs and Crime (UNODC). 2008. Threat of Narco-Trafficking in the Americas. Vienna: October 2008.

United Nations Office on Drugs and Crime (UNODC). 2010. The Globalization of Crime: A Transnational Organized Crime Threat Assessment." Vienna: June 2010.

Womer, Sarah and Robert J. Bunker. 2010. "Sureños Gangs and Mexican Cartel Use of Social Networking Sites." *Small Wars & Insurgencies* 21 (1), 81–94.

The "Criminal Gang," a French Ectoplasm?[1]

François Haut

By way of all-too-frequent news of crime, and sometimes the death of courageous innocents, we have observed a steady increase in the harmful effects of street gangs in France.

And yet a journalist can begin an article on gangs in France as follows: "These are not the armed gangs of Harlem or of the Bronx of yesteryear." How can we claim in this way to be some kind of "French exception," when all the facts show the opposite to be the case?

For thirty years, we have repeatedly been told that the situation "is not like that in the United States," that it is a matter of "sporadic occurrences." We have been repeatedly told that it involves "nonorganized groups" that are spontaneous and volatile, even though homicides, a visible sign of turf wars, and fierce competition, are on the increase, thus demonstrating the structured character of these groups and the sophistication of their trafficking.

This common perception of the phenomenon is false. It is not "youths" who kill each other with Kalashnikovs and then burn the cars in which they dump the bodies; it is thugs, *affidés*[2], and criminal gangs who settle their conflicts of interest with their usual instruments of negotiation—not mere ectoplasms.

This criminality has been brushed under the carpet for years, because it calls into question the dogmas of exonerating penal policies and it disturbs because it is close to home for much of the population. It has only recently been taken into account in France, but is it really serious? It is hard to be sure whether the realities of the phenomenon are appreciated; this is why it is necessary to make them known, so as to reveal more clearly criminal practices that are little known and even less well understood. Here is an illustration.

Shitland

The Police closed "Shitland" on October 14, 2011. Shitland was not an amusement park. It is the name that a gang had given to "its" territory, which was transformed into a supermarket for drugs and systematically bled dry; for years, the inhabitants of the neighborhood of Les Boullereaux in the Champigny-sur-Marne city had been subjected to the predations of the gang, living in an atmosphere of fear and intimidation and enduring the presence of aggressive junkies in need of their fix.

The gang, whose "hardcore" was familial, took possession of four tower blocks in the neighborhood and established a considerable traffic of cannabis in them. This gang had three cousins as its leaders: one of them lived in the Basque country, from where he shipped out most of the merchandise, delivered on an express basis by professional drivers from outside the group, who transported the drugs in large, stolen cars. The other two oversaw the operations at Champigny. As soon as they arrived, the

---

[1] Ectoplasm: a being without consistency, of a substance a little more visible than that of a phantom.

[2] *Affidé*— A gang member in French. The definition of the word given by the Petit Robert dictionary corresponds precisely to the almost legally binding relationship, the bond of blood between an individual and his gang: "one who can be trusted to be ready for any escapade . . . an accomplice ready for anything." We will use here the usual american terminology : *gang member, gangbanger, homie…*

drugs were repackaged into "commercial" quantities in a dedicated apartment in the town.

Buyers came from the entire Parisian region—Shitland had a reputation for the quality of its merchandise. Up to five hundred "clients" a day could be handled, and sometimes queues formed at the foot of the buildings.

The junkies, Shitland's "consumers" in a sense, were escorted from the ground floor of the tower blocks, and led toward the dealer of the day, situated, for strategic reasons, on the sixth or seventh floor of the twenty-story blocks. According to investigators, upon entry, the consumers could read the inscription "Welcome to Shitland." Higher up there was another, reading "Prepare and show your banknotes." Further on, there was a warning: "Fake banknotes = down to the basement for punishment." The clients were then searched, before finally meeting the person who would hand over the precious product for which they had gone to so much trouble. This individual was hooded up and hidden behind (stolen) street furniture to protect him against potential aggressors.

On the upper floors were the wet nurses—that is, residents of the building who kept stocks of drugs in their apartments, and were paid around two thousand euros per month for doing so. And higher still, "squatted" apartments that could serve as a backup in case of a raid by the police.

Gangbangers, usually kids, positioned on mattresses on each floor, were paid around three hundred euros a night to keep watch and tip off about any possible police activity. And to make access difficult and hold up the progress of "invaders," the traffickers had painted the windows in the communal areas black, and wrapped the lights in dark duct tape; there was even a plan to tip oil down the staircases, just in case.

As for the residents of the area, they had to pay ten euros if they wanted to use the elevator, or else hand over a part of their shopping in order to be allowed into their own homes.

During the trial of some members of this Shitland gang in April 2013,[3] the prosecuting attorney recounted "a system of terror" when describing the life of the inhabitants, speaking of an area "where threats and violence were an everyday occurrence." And then there was the trafficking, which, according to police informers, generated a "turnover" of around thirty thousand euros a day.

Can we still say that this is not a matter of organized crime, when we see coming together here all the symptoms of a true criminal organization?

Recipe for a Criminal Genre

The "street gang" is a primitive, collective, and organized criminal genre that has manifested itself with varying intensity throughout history. The gang has been known since way back, from ancient Rome to seventeenth-century London. In Europe, the contemporary version of this criminal phenomenon, inspired by the US model, first began to affect France around the middle of the 1980s.

Since that time, comparable phenomena have been observed in Spain, in Great Britain, in Belgium, in the Scandinavian countries, and in the north of Italy. And with current means of communication and circulation, the genre continues to extend itself.

---

[3] In fact there were two trials, a week apart. Sentences of up to six years of imprisonment were passed for "traffic in narcotics" and "criminal conspiracy." The general atmosphere was confused, because the general opinion was that the main ringleaders were absent.

This form of organized criminality obviously exists in the United States and elsewhere in the world: in South Africa, in the Philippines, in Thailand, in South America; in Central America, it has attained unimaginable proportions.

What is the recipe for a criminal gang? Its essential ingredients are three in number. Two of them are symptomatic of the existence of the phenomenon, whereas the third is pathological:

– A territory that is claimed and dominated, with all that follows from this;
– Specific manifestations and forms of expression, only certain aspects of which are found in France;
– A criminogenic behavior that the English-speaking world calls gangbanging, a word that has no equivalent in French.

• A gang emerges from a territory that it dominates. The territory is the initiating and federative element of the street gang, in the United States and in France alike. This territory is the geographical extent of the gang's physical and "commercial" grip. In France, this territory is generally a "town" or a "neighborhood."

On "its" territory, the gang makes sure that an atmosphere of fear and intimidation reigns. This is what Americans call, and what we should also call, "street terrorism:" terror, in the primary sense of the word—exactly what the prosecutor deplored during the Shitland trial.

Not only is this domination cruelly felt by the inhabitants of the zone, but it is often visible, and thus symptomatic of the appearance or of the existence of a gang. The territory is delimited by graffiti: this trait is common to all gangs in the world, thus making this visibility symptomatic.

The appropriation of a territory brings about the behavior of the gang, its "rules of engagement" on the street. As it is the foundation of the constitution of the gang, it is theoretically sacred: territory must be respected. This means that the gang has to respond to all provocations of which it or its members might be the object, and is thus led into violent confrontations whose causes are rarely clear, and which are becoming ever more numerous in France, with Marseilles only one case among others.

The "value" of territory—that is to say how much it can yield, through all forms of criminal activity, can be one of these causes, but it is far from being the only one; sometimes these reasons for conflict can seem pointless, like a "sketchy look" or a lack of "respect."

Still, this "sacred" character does not prevent criminal gangs from preying on their own territory; it is this behavior that leads to the street terrorism to which residents are subjected.

It is they, living in this atmosphere of fear and intimidation, who undergo this terror that plagues a territory materially delimited by a gang, having to pay the homies to take the elevator in their own building. Hence the importance of listening to these residents, and maintaining ongoing intelligence and informant operations among them. For it is often only through this criminal intelligence that one can get to know a gang, its importance, its practices, its 'bangers, and really fight against it.

• The gang also generates specific manifestations and characteristic modes of expression.

The gang members are visible, just like the territory. Homies most often have a "high profile"—that is to say, they do not hide their affiliation with the group, unlike most criminal societies; on the contrary, they are proud to be part of it, and show this through codified modes of dress, or tattoos expressing the unshakeable bond with the group. This serves to affirm the prestige of their gang, and they are ready to defend it at any moment.

This visibility is also found in "gangsta rap," an expression of gang psychology, which usually consists of little more than hate, racism, and sexism. "Gangsta rap" is a message of incitation diffused to the masses by a consenting or complicit media, written in a crude, insulting, vulgar language that impregnates a broad public with this subculture of drugs, violence, and hatred. There is no lack of examples. Here is one:

J'aime voir des CRS morts,
J'aime les pin-pon, suivis d'explosions et des pompiers
Un jour j'te souris
Un jour j'te crève
J'perds mon temps à m'dire qu'j'finirai bien par leur tirer d'ssus . . .

[*I like to see a riot squad cop dead,*
I like the sirens, then explosions and fire
One day I smile at ya
Next day I make a hole in ya
Waste my time in tellin' myself I'm'a end up shootin' 'em down . . .][4]

- The criminal pathogeny of the gang is expressed by the American term gangbanging, which covers practices that are identical in France and elsewhere, in particular in the United States. "Gangbanging" is a concept that defines everyday life in a gang. It is the term that brings together the elements that constitute the "criminal career" of a gang member.

In the words of a Los Angeles gangbanger, " 'banging ain't no part time thang, it's full time, it's a career"[5] It consists in hanging out in the street, generally starting very young, and doing "business" (this is what illegal "transactions" are called in French); in always being on the lookout for any opportunity for misdeeds, for there is no criminality specific to gangs. It is a continual grasping of opportunities, and we know obviously that drugs play a central role, above all with the arrival en masse of cocaine in France, the lowering of its price, and its distribution by gangs. It is this that explains to a large extent the normalization of the use of the Kalashnikov: to fight against other gangs so as to protect markets and develop new ones, or to ensure that one is "respected."

This culture brings about the form of gang organization. As we have already noted, we often hear it said in France that gangs are not organized—and above all, "not like in the United States." This is untrue; it is a rejection of reality: the organization of these criminal groups is wholly similar in form and in its fundamental logic. How can tons of drugs circulate and be distributed without any form of organization?

This organization, which rests upon personal bonds, from individual to individual, is arranged like a galaxy;[6] it is not a matter of a vertical hierarchy in the form of a pyramid, the only model that we know in our societies.

The gravitation of the elements of this galaxy around the center, and the cohesion of the whole entity, stem from the

---

[4] Excerpt from "Mafia K'1 Fry" Gangsta rap band, "Violence/délinquance."
[5] According to Tray Ball, a member of the "Eight-Tray Crips," cited in Sanyika Shakur, *Monster: The Autobiography of an LA Gang Member* (New York: The Atlantic Monthly Press, 1993), 107.
[6] A galaxy is a set of stars, dust, and interstellar gas turning around a center, whose cohesion is ensured by the forces of gravitational attraction, and forms a well-defined entity.

intensity of attraction exerted by fascination with the "success" of a leader or of the "hardcore" members.

This organization also rests upon the degree to which the gang member is implicated, and the time he spends with the group, which will allow him to get progressively closer to the center and to indicate his place in relation to power.

Finally, the organization rests upon the permanence and the "sacred" character of the social bond that unites the homie with each other and binds the group together. When dissent appears, it is generally because of some rupture—whether real or imagined—of this bond: it shows that the leaders are replaceable, proof of the durability, even if short-lived, of the organization. It also reinforces the bond through violence and the quest for radicalization that generally brings about the replacement of a weaker leader by a "stronger" murderer.

The adhesion to this form of criminal entity and its durability are thus explained by the desire to become like the leaders who have "succeeded," or even to take their place: there is nothing new here. They become the models of where the gangbanger wants to get to so as to finally hold what he believes to be the keys to life: money and power. Money and "power:" the logic of the gang is primal, simplistic, but effective. It is doubtless for this reason that it succeeds in reproducing itself, even though it is often difficult to profit from the money, and "power" only exists through the group, without which individuals are nothing.

"Gangbanging" also creates a particular relationship with prison. Prison becomes a "criminal university," an obligatory rite of passage for every 'banger who wishes to progress, generating another criminal genre that deserves to be treated separately.

Realism against Gangs

We, observers of criminality at the Department for Research into Contemporary Criminal Threats at the Université Panthéon-Assas, have witnessed the birth and the growth of these "street" criminal phenomena in France, and have alerted the authorities and the public since the debate began during the 1990s. Up until now, we have identified territorial gangs, comparable to those observed in the United States, and examined the way they function and their actions.

There are today many hundreds of gangs in France (somewhere between three and five hundred), but in the absence of any coherent definition, we do not know precisely how to evaluate the exact number. There are thirty-three thousand in the United States, and almost 1.5 million gang members; they are responsible for most of the homicides in the country. What part do French gangs play in criminality and homicides? So far, we do not know.

Not so long ago, we read that it was a matter of groups "consisting of fifteen to twenty youths;" today we are talking about groups that number many hundreds of members, and girl gangs that are also taking the path of extreme violence.

We had to wait until 2004 before the term "gang" was publicly accepted, until June 2009 for the question to be broached in the French Parliament, and until September 2009 for the matter to be seriously and concretely addressed by the minister of the interior. But although what is being done goes in the right direction, it is far from being enough, and the standard texts have a poor comprehension of the matter.

In order for the struggle against gangs to be effective, it is necessary to consider the gang as a specific criminal phenomenon. Accordingly, we must create suitable instruments for understanding, evaluation, statistics, and criminal intelligence. And ultimately we need a specific and appropriate apparatus of enforcement, more qualitative than quantitative, one that above all is able to take into consideration the essentially collective and organized nature of the phenomenon.

Crime and Business

Eric Delbecque[1]

Does Economic Warfare Exist?

Criminal organizations threaten businesses just as much as they threaten states and citizens; but there is also such a thing as "economic warfare," which manifests another face of crime, another type of threat to economic interests. The term may be polemical and somewhat alarming, but the reality it refers to is indisputable. Today's businesses compete hard to capture markets that are increasingly coveted by a plethora of competitors. This has become particularly evident as China, Brazil, and India unleash their enterprises in "Western" markets. And states are also a part of this gigantic commercial competition. In fact, the strategic challenges of tomorrow are predominantly economic. None of the other subjects of confrontation have disappeared, but they rank as secondary priorities in the global arena.

So what concretely lies behind the term "economic warfare?" Many things: industrial espionage, intrusions into or straightforward burglary of research laboratories, the poaching of senior executives (as a form of "hostile recruitment"), attacks on public image, the undermining of leaders, and so forth. But in a word: crime. Its motives certainly vary in form, but they all converge in the expectation of turning a profit.

The manipulation of information, in particular, goes from strength to strength. An interesting example is that of Whitehaven Coal. In January 2013, a certain association, judging their business activities to be too polluting, used the headed paper of a large bank to propagate false information and thus to bring down the stock value of the company.[2] For no apparent reason, the share price recorded a sudden brutal drop of around 10%. Following a suspension of trading, an investigation uncovered the publication of a false memo purportedly from the fourth largest Australian bank, ANZ.

The document appeared to announce the discontinuation of financing facilities (of around a billion euros) for the Maules Creek open-cast mine, one of the largest on the planet (and a crucial site for Whitehaven Coal). The fake memo emphasized "the risks associated with the mine's reputation and with analysis of its profitability, in the current highly volatile climate of the coal export market."[3] The markets, rather feverishly, did not hesitate to react. Once the subterfuge was unmasked, activists from the Frontline Action Group (an environmental association opposed to the mine, which they claimed was dangerous to the environment) admitted to being the true authors of the memo.

Hostile takeovers of businesses also stand out as being among the most sophisticated and dangerous threats of the moment.

---

[1] Head of the department of economic security of the INHESJ (Institut National des Hautes Études de la Sécurité et de la Justice [National Institute for Advanced Studies in Security and Law]).

[2] See Charles Gautier, "Des Écolos en lutte contre une mine se font passer pour des banquiers," *Le Figaro*, January 8, 2013.

[3] Translator's note: Quotation back-translated from the French-language version of this article.

We must finally mention the particular problem of social networks. Today the interactive Web constitutes a potential source of information leaks for businesses, as indicated in the following summary.

The Protection of Businesses' Immaterial Assets: Information Leakage and Social Networks[4]

−1 out of every 7 profiles, all social networks included, is the source of an information leak.

−30% of people publish professional information on the Internet

−58% of people publishing professional information do so on Facebook.

Internal Fraud

The danger often comes from within organizations themselves—beginning with fraud. Let us explore this question through a fictional scenario. Here are a series of exchanges taking place between the brand HERCULE, part of the retail group HERAKLES, and Risk Team (a provider of economic intelligence), following the discovery of a case of internal fraud.

Report on Meeting of February 18, 2012, called by Risk Team:

Following our interview on Tuesday February 14, 2012, with Mr. NÉMÉE and Mr. LERNE, we have been advised of the following:

A tax audit having been carried out on the Nice branch of HERCULE, false invoices, implicating local associations, have come to light. The information has been brought to the attention of the National Tax Fraud Squad. Following the discovery, a tax claim (dated November 14, 2000) has been made against HERAKLES (the company that owns the HERCULE brand). The associations have also turned against HERAKLES. These fraudulent practices are apparently not endemic in the region, since nothing similar had been discovered in Cannes.

Mr. MINOS, the official in charge of the case, wished to go to the Etampes branch (whose manager was appointed in 2010). But because of damages sustained to the files of that store (which were kept in poor conditions and destroyed for the period 2002–2005, and are missing for the period covering 2006–2008 and the second half of 2009), Mr. MINOS agreed to focus on the Amiens branch instead.

In regard to the above, our recommendations are as follows:

− The interview with Mr. DIOMEDE, manager of the Nice branch since 2010, should include a series of precise questions, which we propose to explore with Mr. NÉMÉE.

− It is necessary to audit urgently the Amiens branch, so as to verify various things: the absence of any activity similar to that discovered in Nice, the respect for procedures concerning cash receipts for the associations (on certain products in particular), and the general good conduct of the store in regard to all legal obligations.

---

[4] See the study carried out by IFOP for the Atelier BNP Paribas Group (November, 2010), entitled "Le *Personal branding* au service de la marque" ("Personal Branding in the service of the brand.")

– It is equally essential to prepare the manager of the Amiens branch to be able to satisfy the administration's requests with optimum effectiveness, cooperation, and psychological and behavioral appropriateness.

– Finally, although the Etampes site was not selected in the first stage, it is nevertheless important to proceed with its examination as soon as possible. There is nothing to indicate that it will not be the object of a later investigation. The question of the records remains unclear: although a bailliff's report dated December 28, 2005, testifies to the destruction of the records following bad weather, we must examine the reasons for the absence of any such finding for the second period concerned. This point must be clarified as soon as possible, the branch must be examined to ensure it conforms to regulations, and the classification and conservation of accounting records must in general be evaluated for all HERCULE outlets.

As crisis measures, we suggest the following:

– So as to reassure all branch managers of the confidence necessary for good, healthy working relationships and efficiency, it would be useful to organize an information meeting concerning the administration's investigation into the Nice branch (summarising that, during the carrying out of its work, the tax office responsible has brought to light breaches of certain legal procedures that the HERCULE group has made every effort to ensure are followed by all staff). It is indispensable that we ensure branch managers' continued confidence in the executive committee, which is employing all the means at its disposal to treat this affair calmly, responsibly, and with respect for the law and for the persons involved.

– In addition, it is necessary to use this information meeting to reiterate the procedures that the directors of HERCULE have always indicated to its managers and staff, especially concerning the specific rules around the sale of alcohol to associations (conditions relating to the identification of cash payments, their acceptability above the authorized amounts, and so forth.)

Summary sheet (origin: NÉMÉE):

As detailed in the memo of February 18, 2012, the essential facts of the matter are as follows:

– A tax audit having been carried out on the Nice branch of HERCULE, fake invoices (involving local associations) came to light.

– In accordance with the provisions of article 40 of the Code of Criminal Procedure, the tax office revealed the facts to the local public prosecutor on November 14, 2011.

– These facts were subsequently brought to the attention of the National Economic Investigation Squad. The head of the unit in charge of the file visited another site: Amiens (March 16–18, 2012). The three days he spent there brought no problems to light.

– So as to control further possible developments of this affair, to circumscribe it, and to avoid any major risk of damage to the activities or the image of HERCULE and the HERAKLES group, members of the executive committee have been put in touch with specialists in risk management to shed light on these events, and to assure the tax office that we are taking charge of the situation.

– We have learned the following by sending our representatives to Nice:

- Sales of alcohol to associations accounted for cash receipts of more than one thousand euros, without presentation of a HERCULE card, without verification of the identity of the purchaser, and without mention of vehicle registration numbers. This is contrary to the procedures of HERCULE, in line with the regulations.
- It turns out that under the compromised responsibility of the former director of the store, Mr. DIOMEDE, drinks manager Mr. AUGIAS had covered up this failure of procedure, giving instructions to this effect to the cashiers.

The major risks are as follows:

– The escalation of legal responsibility to the executive committee.

– Media exploitation of the affair.

Faced with these events, we have taken the following steps:

– Preparing the manager of the Amiens branch so as to best reply to the questions of the tax office.

– Checking of the delegation of power between Mr. GERYON, regional director during the period concerned, and Mr. DIOMEDE. Currently, it appears that criminal liability in regard to the delegation goes no further than the level of the director of the establishment—that is, Mr. DIOMEDE.

– Initiating a process of internal communication beginning with the last works committee (reiterating the regulations in force with respect to the opening of accounts for associations, cash receipts, and other modes of identification of payers for cash payments), with the aim of:

- Reassuring staff so as to avoid rumours
- Reminding staff of the directors' ongoing concern (as testified by earlier circulars [annexed to the works-committee report]) for compliance with legislation (including that relating to the conservation of records required by the tax office).

The actions underway or being planned are enumerated below:

– A series of interviews with (current and former) staff of the Nice branch.

– An audit of the Estampes branch, which is likely to be visited by the tax office (in particular, to verify the proper maintenance of accounting records).

We have a strong position in relation to the tax office in regard to the following:

1. All identifiable and useful facts relating to the affair have been put in good legal order, so as to give the judicial authorities every assurance of good faith and transparency on the part of the directors of the HERAKLES/HERCULES group on the national and executive level.

2. The results of the internal audit that would permit the group (at the correct moment, if necessary) to itself bring a civil action in regard to the actions of certain of its delegates (namely, Mr. DIOMEDE) and the consequences of those actions, have already been compiled, and will continue to be compiled as the internal inquest progresses.

3. The involvement of Risk Team, an external service provider, to guide the approach to internal information, which, to the eyes of the tax office, evidences a will to clear up the affair, not to suppress it.

Counterfeiting

Counterfeiting is a veritable scourge for business today. Already confronted with increased competition, they must also confront this illegal production which diminishes their market share, threatens jobs, and inevitably degrades their brand image. When this problem is mentioned one usually thinks of its impact upon the luxury industries that were its first victim. In this regard, French brands figure amongst the most counterfeited in the European Union in the domain of cosmetics, perfumes, clothing, and so forth.

However, for some years now counterfeiting has not been limited to the luxury sector alone. It has undergone a definite change of direction toward everyday consumer products. No company is safe from it any longer. The story of a certain Saint-Étienne-based SME, a shoe manufacturer, is particularly revelatory. The commercial site of the brand Archiduchesse.com, 70% of whose sales are transacted over the Internet, was hacked by a Chinese outfit, including its content, logo, and images (including the photo of the French manager). A complete, faithful copy of the French site offers counterfeit versions of the of the SME's products for sale at a sixth of the price. "At the moment this has no impact for us since this site's sales seem to be limited to Chinese markets, but if it were to be translated into French, the counterfeit products could potentially be sold in France, and that would be the end of us,"[5] said the manager of the SME, Patrice Cassard.

It is thus quite clear that counterfeiting can have devastating effects on SMEs (which constitute 70% of the French economic fabric). What is more, in the face of this criminal phenomenon, SMEs are at a disadvantage relative to larger companies.

Any tackling of the problem presupposes the prior putting into place of a monitoring system so as to detect acts of counterfeiting. Before being able to mount any kind of response to defend one's rights, one must firstly know that one is a victim. In addition, launching a legal procedure implies significant expenses, which are often difficult to afford for SMEs. In a case like that of the Archiduchesse brand, the manager of the company would have to spend around fifty thousand euros to appeal to a bailliff to observe the counterfeit production, and then appoint a lawyer to fight the case.

Counterfeiting is a polymorphous phenomena that covers many different economic and legal situations. From a strictly legal point of view, the term "counterfeiting" refers to the violation of intellectual property rights (such as a patent, brand, designs, and models), but in its everyday sense it designates broadly the whole range of acts of parasitism, imitation, and unfair competition. What is more, this polymorphous

---

[5] "Contrefaçon: une entreprise de chaussettes démunie," *Le Figaro*, April 19, 2012, http://www.lefigaro.fr/societes/2012/04/19/20005-20120419ARTFIG00662-contrefacon-une-entreprise-de-chaussettes-demunie.php.

character is illustrated by the existence of different types of counterfeiting: namely, the "fake-fake," fabricated with the incorrect raw materials, the "fake-true," made with authentic raw materials and imitating or reproducing a product partly or totally, without the authorization of the holder of the intellectual property rights; and finally the "true-fake," a product identical to the original, sometimes manufactured in the same factories, and sold directly through a dishonest subcontractor, without the originator's being aware of it. All of which allows us to appreciate more clearly the complexity of the struggle against counterfeiting.

This criminal market is still poorly known and probably underestimated. Although it is difficult to evaluate a market that is by definition invisible, numerous reports published in recent years estimate the turnover of counterfeiting at around five hundred billion euros per year (that is, between 7 and 10% of global commerce).[6] Besides this, we see channels of counterfeiting becoming truly professionalized, a development accentuated by the possibilities offered by the Internet. This phenomenon has today become an industry in its own right. At the other end of the chain, counterfeit commerce costs two hundred thousand jobs every year in Europe, thirty thousand of which are in France.[7] Consequently, the struggle against counterfeiting activity is a crucial challenge for the protection of businesses.

However, beyond the gigantic losses suffered by the economic actors and by the populations of the territories where they are based, counterfeiting above all poses grave problems in terms of security and public health. Numerous counterfeit products prove to be dangerous or even deadly. This is particularly the case with contraband cigarettes manufactured in the Chinese provinces (which contain scraps of fabric or plastic that are hazardous to health) and counterfeit medicines (false viagra), as well as food products (adulterated alcoholic drinks) or spare parts for aeronautics.

A Laundry List of Threats

Of course, the threats described above do not represent an exhaustive list. There are numerous other dangers we have not yet mentioned. An EDHEC study on malevolent acts committed against businesses (based on a survey carried out in eighty-two large European, American, and Japanese companies) revealed the following "hit parade" among the attacks listed:

- 84%: thefts of product and equipment
- 67%: internal fraud
- 39%: hacking into information systems and piracy
- 34%: armed attacks
- 33%: identity theft of businesses
- 17%: kidnapping and hostage taking
- 7%: murder of employees
- Two cases of maritime piracy

So there is no lack of subjects. Beginnng with racketeering (particularly widespread in the waste-processing industry), we should note in particular that its most elaborate form today is piracy in public procurement contracts. This involves control over the awarding of a contract (and thus necessitates a strong collusion with local political authorities).

As for the theft of merchandise, it is concentrated in cargo theft (electrical appliances, perfume, wines and spirits, textiles,

---

[6] Alain Bauer and Christophe Soullez, *Une Histoire criminelle de la France* (Paris: Odile Jacob, 2012).
[7] Mickaël Roudaut, "Crime organisé: un acteur global," in *Sécurité Globale* 5 (Fall 2008).

telephony, delicatessen foodstuffs, and so forth). Very well organized gangs (drawn from itinerant criminals or urban criminal groups) are the principal culprits. The technique consists of diverting convoys or stealing tons of merchandise from warehouses (acting on inside information).

Misappropriation in general also grabs the attention. It manifests itself in three forms:

– Money laundering (mafias and South American cartels)

– The diversion of logistical capacities to criminal ends (triads and Turkish and Albanian mafia can utilise regular road traffic to transport drugs or clandestine migrants across Europe).

– Counterfeiting (misappropriation of technical knowhow or of a brand). The Chinese triads and Russian criminal and terrorists organizations are particularly active in this domain (counterfeiting of luxury goods, pharmaceuticals, textiles, CDs, agribusiness, and aeronautics).

Certain zones of the world accumulate specialities. For instance, the Gulf of Guinea seems to be a particularly difficult space for the petrol industry. This industry exploits the oilfields situated in Nigeria (where 10% of Shell's annual production takes place). So-called "ethnic" criminal action (above all the doing of young people given alcohol, drugged, or conditioned by witchcraft rituals) is a regular reality here. This violence comes from the communities surrounding the extraction zones (which are, it is true, victims of runaway elite corruption and of a glaring inequality in the distribution of the petrol profits). The offending acts (understood and undertaken as a form of pressure or lobbying) aim to obtain the recruitment of laborers or their being kept on in the job after the end of projects. The action of these ethnic gangs has proven particularly brutal in the Niger Delta, which has seen regular attacks on sites, the boarding of barges and platforms, and the abduction and assassination of expatriate staff.

As can be readily seen, these various crimes can easily be enumerated one by one, like an eclectic laundry list. What is said above does not aim to furnish a complete catalogue, but to draw attention to what are now strategic threats for businesses, seriously jeopardizing their development and sustainability.

Made in the USA
San Bernardino, CA
25 July 2014